Critical Pedagogy

Critical Pedagogy
Notes from the Real World

Joan Wink
California State University, Stanislaus

 LONGMAN

An imprint of Addison Wesley Longman

New York • Reading, Massachusetts • Menlo Park, California • Harlow, England
Don Mills, Ontario • Sydney • Mexico City • Madrid • Amsterdam

Critical Pedagogy: Notes from the Real World

Longman, 10 Bank Street, White Plains, N.Y. 10606

Acquisitions editor: Virginia L. Blanford
Production editor: Ann P. Kearns
Editorial Assistant: Michael Lee
Cover design: David Levy
Text art: Fine Line Inc.
Production supervisor: Edith Pullman
Compositor: Digitype

Library of Congress Cataloging-in-Publication Data

Wink, Joan.
    Critical pedagogy : notes from the real world / Joan Wink.
        p.   cm.
    Includes bibliographical references and index.
    ISBN 0-8013-1669-3
    1. Critical pedagogy — United States.   I. Title.
    LC196.5.U6W54   1997
    370.11'5 — dc20   95-50926
                                                            CIP

1 2 3 4 5 6 7 8 9 10-MA-0099989796

Credits

Text credits in order of occurrence:

P. 25, from *Life in Schools: An Introduction to Critical Pedagogy in the Foundations of Education* (p. 169), by P. McLaren, 1989, White Plains, NY: Longman. Copyright 1989 by Longman Publishers USA. Reprinted with permission.

P. 64, from *The Pedagogy of Hope: Reliving Pedagogy of the Oppressed*, by P. Freire, 1994, New York: Continuum Publishing Group. Copyright 1994 by the Continuum Publishing Group. Reprinted with permission.

P. 66, from *Literacy: Reading the Word and the World* (pp. 124–125), by P. Freire and D. Macedo, 1987, South Hadley, MA: Bergin & Garvey. Reprinted with permission of Greenwood Publishing Group, Inc., Westport, CT. Copyright © 1987.

P. 71, from *Social Linguistics and Literacies: Ideology in Discourses* (p. 31), by J. Gee, 1990, Bristol, PA: Falmer Press. Copyright 1990 by the Falmer Press. Reprinted with permission.

P. 90, from "Portrait of John Goodlad," by M. Goldberg, 1995, *Educational Leadership, 52,* p. 85. Copyright 1995 by the Association for Supervision and Curriculum Development. Reprinted with permission.

P. 98, from *Minority Education: From Shame to Struggle* (p. 390), by T. Skutnabb-Kangas and J. Cummins, 1988, Philadelphia, PA: Multilingual Matters. Copyright 1988 by Multilingual Matters. Reprinted by permission.

P. 103, from *Reading Paulo Freire: His Life and Work* (p. 6), by M. Gadotti (1994), Albany: State University of New York Press. Copyright 1994 by State University of New York Press. Reprinted with permission.

P. 118, from "Shifting the Paradigms of Education and Language Policy: Implications for Language Minority Children," by H. S. Garcia, 1993, *The Journal of Educational Issues of Language Minority Students, 12,* p. 4. Copyright 1993 by Boise State University. Reprinted with permission.

P. 148, from "Caring Spells Career Success for the Teacher," by D. Hanson, August 27, 1994, *The Turlock Journal,* pp. A1-A16. Copyright 1994 by Turlock Journals. Reprinted with permission.

P. 148, from "Voices of Reason and Compassion," by R. Elam, March 3, 1995, *The Modesto Bee,* p. A11. Copyright 1995 by The Modesto Bee. Reprinted with permission.

P. 157, from "The Public Curriculum of Orderly Images," by E. Vallance, 1995. *Educational Researcher, 24* (2), p. 84. Copyright 1995 by the American Educational Research Association. Reprinted with permission.

Dedication

To the Prairie People I love
To the memory of my dear Uncle Bob

Contents

chapter **2**

Critical Pedagogy
  What in the World Is It?   17

chapter 3

Critical Pedagogy
   Where in the World Did It Come From?   63

chapter 4

chapter **5**

Critical Pedagogy
Why in the World Does It Matter?   145

Preface

I began teaching in 1966. I came from the rural Midwest and started teaching in a school on the Mainline of Philadelphia. The school was new and huge. Every wall was entirely made of glass windows, floor to ceiling. I could stand in my room and see over the heads of students in many other classes. When the principal was coming down the hall, we knew well in advance. I would like to say that I was a day ahead of each class, but the truth would be more like five minutes. I thought I would teach a lot; I learned more.

I had come from a background of English and Spanish literature and grammar. In my first year of teaching I had to use the audio-lingual method to teach four different levels of high school Spanish. We were to spend six hours a day speaking Spanish—repeating Spanish. One problem: I didn't speak Spanish. I could conjugate any verb in any tense, and I could cite multiple poetic and literary allusions, I just couldn't speak, nor understand, Spanish very well. It seemed like everything I had learned in college didn't fit, an experience I have had several times since. My most vivid memory of my first year of teaching is a continual headache. I swore I would never teach again. I have been teaching and learning ever since. Before I finished my first year, I was able to articulate one concept that had impressed me more than any others: Teachers who teach in glass schools should not throw stones.

My purpose is not to throw stones. My purpose is to look again and to see in new ways. My purpose is to think new thoughts that are applicable to critical teaching and learning for the twenty-first century. I do not teach the way I taught in 1966; I do not learn the way I learned in 1966; I do not believe the way I believed in 1966; I do not know in the way I knew in 1966. My ways of knowing come from my experiences with living, learning, and teaching since that time.

If I were to describe my ways of knowing, I suspect I would say they are holistic (I want to see the whole puzzle first), gender-based (being a mom has taught me more than I can yet understand), linguistic (I love languages), and pluralistic (the "other" anything fascinates me). There you have it — the mystery is gone.

Truthfully, I have not liked learning all I have learned. On this path I have been known to deny, to resist, and to object. I remember a teacher/ friend who said to me in the late 1960s, "Joan, some teachers hurt some kids." My reaction? Blasphemy! Anti-American! Anti everything I had ever taken for granted. Since that time, I have come to learn that sometimes everything my teacher-friend said is true. But, before you throw this book, let me assure you that there is not a mistake in teaching and learning that I have not made. I shudder when I think back on some of my former students, particularly those in that audio-lingual experience. Most survived, in spite of me. I continue to be challenged with my teaching. It seems that sometimes I am a good teacher; sometimes I am a great teacher; and, sometimes I am not so great. Probably this is true of many, many teachers.

THE PURPOSE

Education is in trouble. Much of what we are doing is not working. The purpose of this book is to provide access to the theory and practice of critical pedagogy, which I believe raises new questions and seeks new answers for schools of today. I also hope that this little book will help all educators to know that they really can make a difference.

THE AUDIENCE FOR THIS BOOK

This book has been written for people who care about schools. All are welcome to the dialogue of critical pedagogy.

ORGANIZATION

I have always been intrigued by the way people read books. Many people start at the beginning and read until the last page. This has always amazed me because I rarely read a book like that. I almost always start at the end. I read the bibliography first to see who the author is reading. Next, I read the last chapter. Then, I rove through the pages, savoring each one. I search for treasures in new books. It is only after I am acquainted with the whole of the book, do I begin to read from beginning to end. Even then, I almost always read wherever I want. I reorganize the book according to my own needs.

How to Read This Book

Start on the first page and read until the end. If you do not do this, you will not understand the references, which are developed sequentially. For example, Jonathan begins the book; we will continue to learn from him and other students and teachers throughout the book. Hopefully, this will be the first and only instance that I say, "Do as I say, not as I do."

When I sat down at the blank computer screen to begin this book, I wanted a story that showed (rather than told) of the need for a critical perspective. In the Introduction, you will notice that all I believed didn't work; and, what I didn't believe, did work. Why should I ask you to reflect critically, if I don't? The story of Jonathan is an example of how I try to use the theory of critical pedagogy to reflectively problem pose in my own life. The story of Jonathan is an example of the many educational contradictions that each of us experiences. You are invited to construct, reconstruct, and deconstruct your own "lessons" from this story. I am still working on mine.

The story of Jonathan led me to reflect on those who have taught me that which is the basis of chapter 1, "Critical Pedagogy: How in the World Did I Get into This?" In this chapter I discuss the students who taught me that much of critical pedagogy is discovered in that enlightened, and often uncomfortable, space of relearning and unlearning. In chapter 2, "Critical Pedagogy: What in the World Is It?" I share how my prior knowledge of Vygotsky became a tool for my understanding of the language and thoughts of critical pedagogy. Eventually, I was able to generate meaning from the perspective of real teachers in real classrooms, who are teaching and learning with real students. In chapters 3 and 4, we look at the history and the how-to of critical pedagogy. Chapter 3, "Critical Pedagogy: Where in the World Did It Come From?" traces the roots of critical pedagogy to Latin America, Europe, and North America. This history is enriched with personal anecdotes from some of the leaders who have touched my life. Their theoretical legacy is portrayed as it turns into practice with classroom and community vignettes. Chapter 4, "Critical Pedagogy: How in the World Do You Do It?" shows the reader how to apply the ideas of critical pedagogy in her own classroom, and in her own life. Chapter 5, "Critical Pedagogy: Why in the

World Does It Matter?" offers a glimpse of some of my own emerging answers and offers the readers the opportunity to discover critical pedagogy in the context of their own lives.

DISTINGUISHING CHARACTERISTICS

Throughout the book, I will tell stories. Many of the stories I have lived. Other stories have been told to me by graduate students and teachers whom I have known. I have collected these ethnographic descriptions for many years. All stories are true. I did not make up any of these vignettes. Many of the stories have been decontextualized to protect the guilty. At times, I have changed names, ages, school sites, etc., but the central core of the experience has been maintained. Other times, and with permission, I have used the real names of the participants.

In this book I have linked theory to practice by providing classroom vignettes that demonstrate what theory might look like in real life. You will discover that some of the vignettes will bring a smile to your face. For example, a graduate student/teacher, Lisa, recently shared this story with me.

> *I went to a state preschool conference and had a wonderful time listening to a national authority on preschool education and emergent literacy. The presenter told many delightful stories of her experiences. One that I remember is:*
>
> *A first-grade teacher asked the students to share a "happy thought" every day with the class. This activity is designed to generate language, thoughts, and new experiences. As the children learn new words, they will learn new thoughts. One day a little girl stood up in front of the room and immediately captured the teacher's attention.*
>
> *"I'm pregnant," the six-year-old proudly announced.*
>
> *"What makes you think that?" the teacher cautiously asked.*
>
> *"Well, this morning my mommy said to my daddy that she is pregnant and my daddy said that is a happy thought."*

Other times, the classroom vignettes tell an important story about the hidden educational processes of which we are all a part. Classroom and school experiences also can be a reflection of hidden beliefs turning into behaviors; theory turning into practice; philosophy playing out before our eyes. Another graduate student/teacher, Shari, recently wrote on one of her assignments, "Just like with our vignettes; it's not really what they are saying, but what they mean." For example, in the following vignette, what is the real meaning behind what this educator is saying?

People who are familiar with sports terminology will have heard the expression "put a little English on it," meaning to hit the ball in such a way that it has a certain spin. No matter what position we hold in education, no matter what theories we say we espouse, our beliefs have a way of making themselves known via our casual conversation and our actions. Even when we don't recognize our own beliefs, others can sometimes see them in our behaviors.

The following conversation was heard in an Office of Bilingual Education in a school district. The joke teller is a school administrator and is married to the director of Bilingual Education. Both are monolingual English speakers. The two were visiting one day and asked the following question of those who were gathered in the office.
"How are a Mexican and a golf ball alike? Answer: The harder you hit them, the more English you get out of them."

What theoretical framework is driving the practice of this educator? How does this practice affect kids in schools? How does the theory and practice of *this* educator affect Mexican Americans in *this* school? What should we do about it? The purpose of this text is to look and relook at beliefs and behaviors.

In this book, we will see school experiences through the lens of critical pedagogy. When I began teaching, I saw schools through the lens of behaviorism. I no longer see that way. When you are finished with this book, I do not expect you to think, to know, and to see the way I do. I would hope that you have reflected critically on your own theory and practice and understand your own perspective better.

I do not want every page of this book to be affirming to all. I do want to prod and to poke a tad; I want you to think and to rethink and to unthink. I want you to relate your new thoughts to the context of your life and your experiences.

HOW THE BOOK CAN BE USED

First, this book is meant to be read. Second, I hope you discuss your ideas with a friend. Vygotsky and I would love it if you did. Third, I hope you write as you read. I want you to scribble your thoughts and ideas in the boxes that are provided and in the margins of the book. I suspect some of you may want to buy a new blank journal so you can write along with me as you read.

I also think this text would make a good little book for those in teacher education, language and literacy, and multicultural education. I suspect that the departments of social-cultural-historical foundations and philosophy will also find it interesting.

Ultimately, my wish for this little book is that it will be found, worn and tattered, lying around on coffee tables, in teachers' lounges, on kitchen counters, and in backpacks.

ACKNOWLEDGMENTS

For many years I have socially constructed the contents of this book with the help of my family and friends. Your conversations and ideas have transformed me as a teacher and learner. Thank you.

Ginny Blanford's quiet support throughout the preparation of this manuscript gave me courage. At one point when I shared some of my most delicate and fragile thoughts, she told me what I needed to hear, "Just write it." Travis Lester saved me from myself at crucial moments with her delightfully jarring editorial comments. Peter McLaren opened the right door to the right office when I was still looking for the right building. Kristen Little read an early draft and asked me hard questions. When I could not answer her questions, I pushed the delete key. Tove Skutnabb-Kangas and Mem Fox have taught me to write honestly.

I am indebted to many graduate students and teachers who arrive exhausted and hungry for our evening classes. I would be discouraged with the state of public education if I were not able to hear their powerful stories of teaching, learning, loving, and caring. I know I am entering into dangerous areas by naming just a few of the graduate students who have read and reread my writing, but special thanks go to Cathi, Donna, Jan, Manuel, Meg, Laura, Sarah, Shirley, and Terry. My friends Sharon and Janet continue to support, encourage, and affirm my work — something that all learners and teachers need.

I am indebted to my friend Yiqiang Wu, who joined with me to write and publish an earlier version of these ideas. The graphics in this document are the result of his computer drawings. Patty Swanson and I previously published some of the ideas regarding lesson plans. LeAnn Putney, Irma Bravo-Lawrence, and I have presented and published some of these thoughts about Vygotsky. Thank you to these very special friends.

To Longman's reviewers, who took time to read and respond quickly and critically, I am indebted. You have sharpened my language and my thoughts:

Lawrence J. Dennis — Southern Illinois University
Christian Faltis — Arizona State University

John Georgeoff — Purdue University

Thomas Jamison — Appalachian State University

Stephen D. Oates — Northern Michigan University

Peggy Placier — University of Missouri

Richard E. Rasmussen — University of Wisconsin/Lacrosse

Francisco Rios — California State University/San Marcos

Susan J. Rippberger — Youngstown State University

John C. Stansell — Texas A&M University

James K. Uphoff — Wright State University

To my colleagues at CSUS — thank you for making me feel like I belong.

To Dean, Dawn, and Bo, who have walked down this unlearning path with me. This book is a celebration of us.

And, to those Benson kids! They are the ones who taught me to learn, to relearn, and to unlearn. I went to Benson, Arizona, in the mid-1970s thinking, "I will teach; they will learn." It seemed so simple. It was not. They taught me that teaching is learning.

Introduction

The Story of Jonathan

I learned to read by way of phonics in the first grade. First, I learned the individual letters and their sounds; from letters and sounds, I moved to individual words; from words, to sentences, to paragraphs, to pages, to stories. I learned to read by building up the parts; bottom to top. Reading specialists would say I was a parts-to-whole reader. Some would say that phonics gets the credit. I slowly and carefully put the puzzle together piece by piece. In school I read every assignment, every chapter, every set of comprehension questions at the end of chapters, every spelling list, every grammar assignment. I read everything I was told to read; I got good grades and graduated at the top of my high school class. One problem: I hated to read. I read only the exact number of pages assigned; I never took a book home to read for pleasure. I went to college and continued the same pattern. I spent every free moment in the library, got good grades, graduated with honors in literature, and yet I still hated to read.

When my children were babies, I started to read to them. The baby books said I should, so I did. With our first child, Dawn, something started to change: I loved the big black-and-white checkered book, *The Real Mother Goose*. I thought *Winnie the Pooh* had been written just for me. By the time we got to *Charlotte's Web*, I was hooked on books. I used to secretly read *The Secret Garden* even when Dawn was asleep. With our son, Bo, I broadened my literary base. I probably have read *The Three Little Pigs* several thousand times, and I still huff and puff with vigor. *Pecos Bill* was the highlight of Bo's preschool years at home. From there he moved on to BMX magazines, and we both became authorities on racing bikes. After BMX magazines, he moved on to motorcycle books. From there, he jumped right into Stephen King and left me far in the dust. It was at this point in my life that I had to find my own books to read. I was probably about thirty years old.

When did Dawn and Bo learn to read? I have no idea, but it was before kindergarten. One day Dawn came home from kindergarten crying because the librarian wouldn't let her check out *The Secret Garden*. The librarian said it was too hard for kindergartners and only third-graders could have it. The same librarian would only let the students check out one book at a time, a rule that Dawn hated. One day she checked out her one allotted book, shoved three more inside her T-shirt, and headed for the exit. She had detention for a week. (This meant that we all had detention for a week, as we lived in the country an hour away from school.)

Dawn and Bo learned to read the opposite way that I did. Reading specialists would say that they were whole-to-part readers. They looked at the picture of the whole puzzle first and then put the pieces together. Do they love to read? Yes. Do they read for pleasure? Yes.

When I first started to notice all of this, it seemed like a contradiction. How could my kids possibly learn to read if they didn't do the same thing I had done? Didn't I need to teach them the sounds, the letters, the words first? However, it was clear to me that they were not interested in the *parts*. They wanted the *whole* story again and again and again. Since that time, I have been very interested in the various ways that children learn to read and read to learn. This is what triggered my interest in holistic teaching and learning. It seems that many kids who were read to as little children, learn to read and love to read. Homes with books and ideas and love seem to produce kids who love to read — except for Jonathan, who is a 12-year-old contradiction in my educational space.

Jonathan comes from an enriched family. He has food, love, and lots of laughs. His dad is an international lung specialist; his mother is the best-read person I know; and, his brothers and sisters are (usually) good to him. Now that I am at a point in my life where I philosophically understand why kids with books learn to read, I must still be alert to the exceptions. I listen to the whispering of the juxtaposition.

Jonathan spent two years of preschool in a two-way Spanish-English immersion where 50 percent of the students were English speakers, and 50 percent of the students were Spanish speakers. His two oral languages grew rapidly. Jonathan flourished as he ran and played in this bilingual context. When he spoke to the English role model teacher, he used only English. When he needed something from the Spanish role model teacher, he switched to Spanish without hesitation. In class and on the playground, he used either language with his peers.

Jonathan entered kindergarten and was able to continue in a two-way immersion program. This program had been well established years ago. The first group of students had already graduated from high school and were now bilingual college students. Some of these students were European Americans; some were Mexican American, but they all were biliterate and all were continuing to achieve academically.

In this program Jonathan had the best of everything: the best teachers, pedagogy, field trips, fish bowls, crayons, and curriculum. Jonathan's prior experiences and this school setting could not have been better. We were ready for Jonathan's emergent literacy to begin.

He didn't read in kindergarten; we waited. He didn't read in first grade; we waited and started to worry. He didn't read in second, nor third, nor fourth, nor fifth grade. I called reading specialists in several states. I read every book on reading I could find. The message consistently was: read to him; talk with him about ideas; love him; give him success in other areas. We did it all. Jonathan's applesauce won a blue ribbon at the state fair. He became an avid photographer and joined a senior citizen's photography club where every member adored him. In his neighbor's garage he developed an interest in and ability in carpentry. But still he couldn't read. We worried more and tried everything: stories, phonics, print-rich environment, dittos, sandpaper letters, Cool Whip sentences, more stories, more love. With each passing year, we became less philosophically grounded and more eclectic. We tried everything I believed in and everything I didn't believe in, and I don't like to admit this to you.

Jonathan's two oral languages continued to grow at a rapid rate. He knew so much, but he couldn't write about it, nor could he read.

Tests. Tests. And, more tests. Jonathan knew every specialist in the district. Jonathan soon began to feel very bad; his self-esteem suffered. His family, his neighbors, and his teachers continued to focus on what Jon could do, and not what he couldn't. But, we were all in agony. The special services division of the district assessed Jonathan with *every* test available. Jon and his parents suffered through interminable student-study-team meetings where each time new well-meaning strangers offered new advice based on yet another test.

Finally, in the summer of his fifth grade, his desperate parents enrolled Jonathan in a private program that focused on auditory discrimination deficit, a problem that several tests had ruled out long ago. The teacher of this program said it would be different. It was. It was prohibitively expensive; the students had to focus for four hours at one sitting; Jon would have to go every day; the parents had to commit to 40 hours minimum.

I was the least optimistic of all. This program was everything that I knew wouldn't work. This was a wreck waiting to happen. I understand why Jonathan's parents were willing to try, but I was confident that this would only do more harm to Jonathan's failing self-concept. He did not need another failure.

After his initial visits, Jonathan called me long distance and excitedly asked me to come and watch him read. I jumped in the car and drove several hours and arrived in time to attend the next session with him. We entered the living room, which had been transformed into a type of reading laboratory for Jon with pictures of tongues and mouths in various positions, manipulatives, cards, and a board that reminded me of a 3-D Monopoly game. Jonathan sat down and focused on the instructions and the sounds he was to make. He knew where his tongue went for every sound. He proudly explained the difference in sounds and talked excitedly about "lip poppers" and "lip tappers." He knew the difference between "fat" sounds and "skinny" sounds; he didn't confuse the "coolers" and the "tongue coolers." By breaking down words into very, very small parts, Jonathan was able to break through the decoding barrier.

"Now, I am finally starting to read, Joan," he proudly told me. For years I have studied the debate regarding whether we learn to read from whole-to-part or from part-to-whole. Does it help us to have a picture of the puzzle before we start to put the puzzle together? Yes. Does it help us to know the story before we begin to read each page, each paragraph, each sentence, each word, each sound? Yes. If families love reading and spend wonderful times reading to their children, will the children begin to read and love to read? Yes. Except for Jon.

Jonathan is now reading and writing in the sixth grade. He sometimes still struggles with spelling tests. Recently, he was trying to memorize the word *aboard*. Jonathan did not know this word; had never used this word, and could see no need for it in his life. He said to his mom, "Even if I learn to spell it by Friday, I still won't know it next Monday."

"Let's move on to social studies," his mom replied, recognizing that he understood far more than how to spell *aboard*. The two of them began to talk about the various people who live in the world, as part of the social studies assignment. Suddenly, Jonathan became very excited and said to his mom, "*People. People*, now there is a word I could really use. I'll learn how to spell *people*, and I'll always know it." He knew it on Friday, and he knew it the following Monday, and he still knows how to spell it.

Jonathan is the whispering of the juxtaposition for me. He is the voice of the *other*. Jonathan teaches me to keep learning from the opposites of my beliefs. After writing this story, I sent a copy to Jonathan and his mom. Jon was delighted to read about himself but disappointed with me.

"Mom, she didn't get it," he groaned.
"What didn't she get?" his mom asked.
"She missed the whole point. The reason I'll always remember
how to spell people *is because I need to know it."*

No, Jonathan, I didn't miss the point. I get it.

CONTRADICTIONS AND CHANGE

Now, why in the world am I beginning a book on critical pedagogy with a story about Jonathan's reading? Critical pedagogy is to literacy as theory is to practice; they are inseparable partners in schools. Since I am a holistic teacher and learner, Jon's inability to read at the prescribed time was an affront to my beliefs. It slowly began to dawn on me that Jonathan and I were living what all those critical pedagogy books called the *other*.

What is the *other*? It is all I haven't experienced. It is what I don't know and understand. It is the upside-down to my right-side-up. For each of us, the *other* is unique. My *other* need not be yours. However, many of us are often uncomfortable with the *other*. The antithesis does not affirm. The *other* asks us questions, and our answers don't fit. This text is filled with stories of the *other* and how students and teachers have reacted to it. I wanted you to see how I reacted when it happened to me.

When Jonathan's parents asked me why he wasn't reading, I tried to explain it away based on my own ways of knowing. Later, I became a desperate eclectic, which I hate to acknowledge. Multiple tests for Jon and lots of specialists had eliminated many possible explanations. My years of observation and reflection had simply used up my literacy knowledge base. The well was dry. Eventually, I had to admit to Jonathan's parents and to myself the truth: I just didn't know why.

Finally, Jon's parents found pieces of the answer in the *other*. Does this mean that all my critical and holistic ways of knowing are bad and wrong? I doubt it. Critical pedagogy has taught me that education is rampant with complexities, contradictions, multiple realities, and change. It has taught me that I don't know everything. I love and hate the Jonathan story.

In my preparation to be a teacher, no one ever told me about contradictions in education. No one ever told me about change in education. However, I am learning that contradictions and change are fundamental for critically teaching and learning in the twenty-first century. Lately, I have been thinking a lot about these two important topics and would like to share my musings with you. Reading books about critical pedagogy forced me to see the contradictions and changes in education — even when I didn't want to see them.

Jonathan is a contradiction in my educational space. My observations and reflections of Jon teach me that:

- I must continually challenge my long-held assumptions;
- I must let practice inform my theory;
- I must continually build theory that informs my practice;
- I must find new answers for new questions;
- I must grapple with multiple ways of knowing;
- I must listen, learn, reflect, and act.

From Paulo Freire and others, I have learned that we all have contradictions in our educational spaces. We all are experiencing fundamental change. We even have oppositional voices in our educational spaces. The trick is to learn from the contradictions, from the change, from the opposite. No one ever said that teaching and learning would be like this. You can imagine my surprise.

Probably, the most important legacy that I have received from my study of critical pedagogy is that all of us need to reflect critically on our own experiences and those of others — then, we need to connect these new thoughts to our own life in new ways. We do not come from a tradition in schools that encourages critical reflection. We, in schools, are often so busy *doing* that we fail to take time for *thinking*. Thinking about important ideas needs some nurturing in our classes. It takes time. The outcomes are not so immediately visible. The outcomes are more difficult to quantify initially. And, it looks like we're not doing anything. However, many of us would agree that what we are doing is not working very well.

Jonathan has made me rethink some of my assumptions about the inherent nature of change and contradiction in teaching and learning. Critical pedagogy has been the impetus that caused me to reflect and read for more understanding of my past and my future.

Many of the contradictions and changes in education cause conflict within each of us. Critical pedagogy has helped me to understand that this is all a natural part of learning. Let's think about it: How can learning possibly be static?! It is inherently grounded in change. I find that when I take time to reflect on the many contradictions and changes, I am more comfortable moving through conflicting feelings and complex understandings. I used to resist; I used to deny; I used to be very uncomfortable whenever I entered this awkward, uncomfortable space of not-knowing. Now, I understand more fully that the many paradoxes and contradictions of education are not as painful when we can articulate all of the change that is swirling around us. In fact, it can even be fun.

"I hate ambiguity," the grad student said to me and her classmates.

"No, we must welcome ambiguity; we must relish ambiguity; we must frolic and play in ambiguity because then we know we are moving along the learning curve," I responded. Since that time, the class and I have had a lot of fun laughing about how much we love and hate this space of ambiguity. The class now recognizes every time we enter its slippery surface.

For me, these contradictions have become the whispering of the juxtaposition. In my educational space, when I bump into a contradiction, I try to imagine the juxtaposition that sits quietly on my shoulder and whispers in my ear to listen and to learn.

This story captures much of what is wrong with education. My process of learning to read was joyless, but I learned. Jon's was joyful, but he didn't learn. I learned because of the accepted traditional approach to reading. The status quo worked for me. Jonathan only learned when we entered into the nontraditional approach, which, at least for me, was very unacceptable. It was only because his parents had the courage and patience to break with the status quo that Jon learned to read. The good news of this story is that Jonathan and I both continue to learn, and finally, we both love to read, even though Jonathan got to that point far earlier in life than I did!

The shimmering differences are what we feel as we continue to walk down our unique learning path; they cause the dissonance we feel when we are at the crossroads of contradiction. At this enlightened — and often uncomfortable — educational space, relearning and unlearning begins.

LOOKING AHEAD FOR ELUSIVE ANSWERS

I, like you, am constantly searching for those very elusive answers. Of course, what I usually discover is just new questions. My intention is to share some of the milestones along my path as I have searched for answers. I don't believe that my answers need to be your answers, but I am confident that by sharing my searching, something that I say may trigger another thought for you in the context of your life and your learning. Throughout the text, the readers are invited to read and write their search for answers with me. The answers we have today are often fleeting because the social, cultural, political, historical context of our lives will change, and tomorrow will be different.

What questions are the most important to you in the context of your life and learning right now?

What are some of your elusive answers?

chapter 1

Critical Pedagogy

How in the World Did I Get into This?

Critical pedagogy has pushed me to reflect on my past and my future. What I have learned from these musings has caused me to see and to know in new ways. The contradictions and the changes have made me stop and rethink what I used to know about teaching and learning.

THE BENSON KIDS: TEACHING IS LEARNING

The truth is that much of what I know about teaching and learning, I learned when I was teaching Spanish and English to junior and high school kids in Benson, Arizona, a rural community in the desert Southwest. Initially, I thought I would teach and they would learn. Gradually and painfully, I began to recognize that my assumptions were wrong. In fact, much of the teaching methodology that I had learned previously just didn't seem to work. Much to the students' dismay, I tried it all: grammar-translation, audio-lingual, direct method, notional-functional, silent way, jazz chants, and, our all-time favorite, total *physical* response. I vividly recall the day in class when I decided you could only throw erasers for so long, and then we needed a little total *mental* response.

Before I tell you all the secrets these students taught me about teaching and learning, let me introduce them to you. I first met many of these students in 1977 when I started teaching the sixth, seventh, and eighth grades in this small school district.

Within the first 24 hours, they started teaching, I started learning. I learned all 28 eighth graders' names and faces only to discover that they had — yes — told me the wrong names. I had other classes but this group was my homeroom class, and I would be spending the majority of my day with them. My new colleagues were quick to warn me about all the "problems" that I had received. The students had many labels, which I have since learned to hate: at risk, troublemaker, problem child, minority, "limited English proficient," and so on. Many of the families lived in areas that we would today call low socioeconomic communities. It seemed to me that they were just families that were working as hard as they could, and doing the best they could, and trying to enjoy their life a little.

I was hired to teach language arts. You must remember that I came from an English literature and Spanish grammar background. When they asked me if I could teach language arts, I thought, "Sure, what could be so difficult? I know about languages and literatures, so I certainly must know about language arts." When I walked into the classroom the first day, I soon learned *what* could be so difficult. There, lined up on a shelf that ran the length of one wall, were all the texts: 28 light-blue spelling books, 28 royal blue basal readers, 28 tan penmanship books, 28 large burgundy grammar books (at last, something I recognized — in fact, I had used it when I was their age), and 28 yellow language arts workbooks. Let's see: $5 \times 28 = 140$ texts for my eighth graders, and I would have other books for my sixth and seventh graders. I knew I would never be able to keep track of all these books, so my first decision was one of the best I ever made: Toss the texts. At that time, I did it out of desperation, but doing so taught me more than several teacher education courses had ever done. The truth is that we didn't really toss the texts; we just left them in nice visible stacks on the shelf in case anyone ever wanted to use them (or, see us using them).

On the second day, one of the boys who was considered by his peers to be among the "biggest and badest" asked a really good question.

> *"If we aren't going to use them books, what are we going to do until June?" Danny, spokesperson of the eighth graders, asked with a hint of challenge in his voice.*
> *"Let's just read and write," I responded.*
> *"Read and write?" they said in unison. "What?"*
> *"Whatever we want," my mouth answered. I can assure you that no one in the room was more surprised than I by my response. But, you must remember that I was just trying to get through the day.*
> *"Anything?" they pushed.*
> *"Anything," I innocently answered.*

That day after school, I drove to Tucson to explore the used book stores. There, on the floor in the back of the store by the gardening books, I found a little worn paperback entitled *Hooked on Books,* by D. N. Fader and

E. B. McNeil, which was published in 1966. I had never heard of Fader, nor McNeil, nor this book, but it seemed right for the moment. I took the book home and read it cover to cover.

Fader and McNeil had some unusual ideas for the times. They said students should read, and then write about their reading in journals. They said teachers should not correct errors, but that I should respond meaningfully to what the students wrote. Not correct grammar and spelling errors?! Heresy. Fader also said students could write anything they wanted, and I was only to assign a specific number of pages, which would increase with each passing week. Quantity over quality, I thought. But, remember, I was desperate. I had 28 faces to face the next day, and they were probably expecting me to have some answers.

On the third day with my students, I told them what I had found, and we discussed their ideas. They agreed to go along with me. During this discussion, I also mentioned to the class that I had just read a journal article that said it really didn't matter if I corrected all their errors. The article said they wouldn't learn from my corrections. I vividly recall Albert, who already had a reputation for his behavior, mumbling for me to hear: "I could have told you that." These were disturbing ideas for me because all I could think about was the enormous amount of time I had wasted correcting students' papers with the great red pen.

In those days we had no idea what a journal was so we just used the school-supplied lined paper, which we placed inside the school-supplied construction paper. The first week, I assigned five full pages, both sides, every line filled. The students were shocked and sure they couldn't do it.

My actions in the classroom were now counter to anything I had ever been taught, but I had gone too far to turn back. The students slowly began to find materials to read; even more slowly they began to write. Danny, of course, was the first to issue a challenge. I noticed the magazine, which in those days we called a "girly" magazine, and knew that every eye in the class was watching. However, my parenting had prepared me for this, and I shot him the ole' "Mom-eye." Today, I would not be so gentle. Today I would grab the magazine and use it for curriculum to demonstrate how little girls and little boys are socialized in different ways in our culture. Danny was lucky; he knew me before I knew about gender biasing.

José was the next to issue a quiet, but direct, challenge. The entire class was busily reading and writing. I was quietly walking among the desks and responding to students. When I came to José, I noticed he was writing rapidly. He had a large book, the Tucson phone book, and he was copying names. Long lists of names filled his blank papers. *Hooked on Books* had prepared me for this. Fader and McNeil told me this would happen. They told me that the student would soon tire of this and would want to move to something that interested him.

> *"What are you writing, José?" I asked.*
> *"I'm copying the phone book," he replied.*
> *"Where are you in the alphabet?" I asked.*
> *"I'm still on the A's," he answered.*
> *"Okay," I said and moved on to the next student.*

José never made it to the B's. From the Tucson phone book, he went right to reading about geography and writing about places he found in the almanac. José eventually graduated with honors in English and in Spanish and is now a pilot in the U.S. military. He has visited most of those places he used to write about.

Each Monday I assigned more pages. Each Friday I went home with a huge stack of messy, dirty construction-paper journals, each filled with treasures and literacy. The next Monday the students got their journals back with my comments, thoughts, questions, and stickers. I remember the absolute joy and delight I saw on the faces of those "problems" when they read my responses on Monday. I finally quit adding more pages when we hit 30 per week simply because I couldn't carry everything. I knew Fader and McNeil were on to something powerful when the kids groaned and complained when our free reading and writing time was over.

Remember the blue basals that had been left on the shelf with the other texts? Eventually they were used by one boy, Gilbert, who read every single story in the blue basal. He not only read every story; he thoroughly enjoyed them. Gilbert had been considered a nonreader who had resisted every basal to date. During the spring months, he continued to explore the texts stacked on the shelf and shared his discoveries with me. I think he thought I should have this information. Upon reflection, I think I was not fooling Gilbert; he knew I needed all the help I could get. I remember in late spring, the students took the annual achievement test. As with several other students, Gilbert's reading scores jumped three grade levels.

> *"What did you do for Gilbert?" the principal asked me.*
> *"What did I do?! What did Gilbert do for himself and for me," I thought to myself.*

The other 27 students and I completely enjoyed the freedom of reading and writing. As the students took control of their own learning, their reading and language scores soared. Gilbert read his texts; the other students read science fiction, history, novels, texts from other classes, and even poetry. I read educational journals. I didn't understand it then, but I do now. From these students, I learned:

> Reading improves writing.
>
> Choice matters.
>
> We get smarter when we write.
>
> We love it when someone responds to our writing.

All my teaching and learning since those years is directly related to my experiences teaching and learning with the Benson kids. We discovered by reading, talking, writing, hearing, experiencing, risking, and musing. We learned together. We learned that it all takes time — the great enemy of public education! Every time I read books about critical pedagogy, I see their faces; I hear their questions; I remember their laughter and tears.

LEARN, RELEARN, AND UNLEARN YOUR WAY TO CRITICAL PEDAGOGY

A group of those students in that sixth grade were in my classes in the seventh, eighth, ninth, tenth, eleventh, and twelfth grades as their classes and my teaching assignments changed. Teaching and learning with this group of students for six years gave me the courage and patience to learn, to relearn, and to unlearn, which eventually led me to a study of critical pedagogy.[1]

To Learn: Difficult Learning Experiences

The Benson students taught me that we learn by reading, talking, writing, listening, experiencing, doing, engaging, interacting, problem solving, problem posing, and taking risks. And, we do it better if we are in a safe and secure environment with an adult who cares about us. Learners choose what to learn. If it doesn't matter to learners, it doesn't matter.

In my own experience, I can remember several learning experiences that were not wonderful. My doctoral course on statistics, for instance; now, there is something that was not fun to learn.

Now that I am no longer teaching and learning with the Benson kids, I want you to know who my current students are. I am teaching in a state university. When I speak of my graduate students, I am talking about people who have been up since 6 A.M., washed a load of clothes, got the kids off to school, taught all day, went to an after-school meeting, and arrived at the university for a night class. Yes, I teach tired teachers. Even though my graduate students seem to be very hardy souls, sometimes I can see that learning isn't always wonderful for them either — for instance, when I tell my grads that they have to learn to use the Internet for our class.

To Relearn: Difficult Relearning Experiences

Learning can be very challenging, but the problem is that it always leads to relearning, which is more challenging. I think that relearning often involves a shift in methodology. When I walked into that Benson class, I had to shift my methodology from what I had learned previously to that which I needed to learn from the students. Relearning takes places when kids teach us all those things we didn't learn in teacher education.

Sometimes the students are far enough along the relearning curve to understand that the ideas we generate in class are not for class only — rather, they are to be applied to their own worlds. For example, María wrote:

> As I start off each new year in teaching, I have to *relearn* because each class is so unique that I can't use the same type of teaching methods or discipline. I never could understand how teachers could come into the first faculty meeting of September and have their lesson plans done for the entire year. Don't we have to base our teaching on the needs of our students?

It's reassuring that in our own struggle with relearning, we are in good company. Paulo Freire criticizes his followers for just being content with his first texts and not reading the critiques he has made of his own work, which show that learning and relearning never end (cited in Gadotti, 1994, p. 88).

To Unlearn: Difficult Unlearning Experiences

Learning and relearning prepare us for unlearning, which is the most challenging. Unlearning involves a shift in philosophy, beliefs, and assumptions. Unlearning is unpacking some old baggage.

When I was a little girl, I learned from my Grandma Grace that the melting pot was a symbol of all that was good. Eventually, I had to unlearn that the melting pot was not so wonderful for everyone; some got burned on the bottom. This experience with unlearning was very uncomfortable because it challenged all my previously held assumptions.

The Sioux Indians, who lived on the reservation two miles away, tried to jump into that pot for the sake of being "good Americans." They tried to talk like Grandma, be like Grandma, think like Grandma, act like Grandma, but no matter what they did, they could not *look* like Grandma. By doing what they had been taught was right and good, they gave up their language, their traditions, their beliefs, and, in many cases, their very souls. When they leaped into that hot pot, far too much was boiled away. I finally came to unlearn that the pot is really about power. The melting pot worked for my Grandma, but not for her neighbors.

As a European American feminist from a prestigious West Coast university recently told me:

> *I have long considered myself to be an enlightened feminist. However, my comfortable framework was ripped out from underneath me when I met, Pam, an African American feminist who consistently points out the multiple ways in which the feminist movement is Eurocentric.*

Unlearning is central to critical pedagogy. Except, it often feels terrible. This is good. Does it feel like everything you ever learned, you now need to relearn and unlearn? This is good. At least for me, it often seems that all I ever held to be true about teaching and learning has been called into question. Many of my long-held assumptions have not stood the test of time.

LOOKING AHEAD FOR YOUR STORIES
OF RELEARNING AND UNLEARNING

As critical pedagogy forces us to shift from passive to active learning, I invite you to reflect, read, and write with me. What have been some of your most difficult relearning and unlearning experiences?

Being a classroom teacher meant that I knew about what went on in the school —
That I can learn from collegial events
That schooling is about power relationships and negotiating

NOTE

1. Learning — Relearning — Unlearning: As you will see, others have discovered and assigned different meanings to relearning and unlearning. However, long before I ever heard of Alvin Toffler, relearning and unlearning had very specific meanings for me based on the context of my own teaching and learning — a good example of generative knowledge. For me, relearning relates to methods. In the 1970s and early 1980s, I was always relearning, relearning, relearning. It seemed that every time I finally knew how to do something in the classroom, I had to relearn it. Relearning can be uncomfortable at first, but eventually, it becomes something we do without thinking. Relearning can be tough, but we know it is doable.

   However, for me, unlearning is something very different. It is fundamentally more painful. It involves a complete reexamination of philosophy, beliefs, and assumptions. It means I have to look seriously at myself and not at others, never a simple task. Unlearning is jumping across the great paradigm. Unlearning took place for me when I moved from behaviorism to transformational teaching and learning. It took decades and not every moment was wonderful. My most recent experience with unlearning is chaos theory, which once again is teaching me that many of my old assumptions about science are dated, or maybe just wrong. Since the mid-1980s, my teaching and learning has involved a lot of unlearning, which leads to more relearning and back to learning: the great cycle of pedagogy.

   Critical pedagogy encourages us to find the magic of personal discovery based on our own lived experiences. Critical pedagogy encourages each of us to reconstruct the words and thoughts of others so that they become meaningful in our own life! Yes, the pattern of learning-relearning-unlearning can be molded and changed and extended to fit your ways of knowing. Critical pedagogy teaches us not to trust prescriptive recipes. In critical pedagogy we read and reread and we write and rewrite. We take ideas and turn them into action. Please take the process of learning-relearning-unlearning and make it fit your ways of knowing and your experiences.

chapter 2

Critical Pedagogy

What in the World Is It?

DAWN *DOES* CRITICAL PEDAGOGY

> *"All the toys are old, broken, and dirty," she said as she burst through the door. Dawn had just returned from her first day of teaching bilingual kindergarten in a district that had never had a bilingual program, although the majority of their students historically came from migrant families who spoke Spanish.*
>
> *"The last teacher left boxes and boxes for my kindergarten students. It's just junk. I snuck out to the garbage and threw it away. There were even teaching materials from the 1950s," she groaned.*
>
> *Dawn was born in 1968. I know; she is my daughter.*

Critical pedagogy teaches us to name, to reflect critically, and to act. In this case, Dawn named it: Junk. She critically reflected, probably as she snuck outside to find the garbage. And, she acted: She tossed it. Critical pedagogy helped Dawn to understand that 40-year-old teaching materials in English would not meet the needs of her Spanish-dominant kindergarten students.

DEFINITIONS

One way to begin this chapter would be for me to list several definitions of critical pedagogy right now. But, no, I will not do that because you might be tempted to memorize any one of them as if it were the *one true* definition.

And, even if you memorize a definition, you'll soon forget it, unless you own it and it matters to you. As Jonathan taught us: "Even if I know *aboard* on Friday, I'll forget it by Monday. But, *people*, now there is a word I could really use."

I would prefer that we move together through these pages until you create a definition that matters to you. I know. It takes longer this way. It is more difficult this way. But, once you have created some meaning for critical pedagogy for yourself, you will never forget it and you will only be able to enrich your meaning as you learn and experience more. So, if you are groaning now, I understand. My grad students understand. They all periodically love and/or hate to learn in this mode of critical pedagogy; it was just so much easier when we could just sit passively and repeat what was transmitted. In using this text, you need to engage actively. If you find an idea you love or one you hate or one you don't understand, call a friend and discuss it until you create some meaning.

Many people (a.k.a. teachers and students) say they just can't write, but they talk very well. Writing is just talking on paper or a computer monitor. If you have trouble writing, just talk with someone or talk with yourself, then just capture what you said on a napkin, scrap of paper, or a journal. Or, go to your computer and start "talking at the blank screen" (some call this writing) until you make some sense of your own thoughts. I used to think that I wrote for a grade, or for an assignment, or for someone else. I have finally figured out that I write (1) so someone will respond to my thoughts, and/or (2) so I can further develop my thoughts. Critical pedagogy has helped me understand that when I write, I am clarifying my own thinking.

Generative Definitions

Generative literacies and generative knowledges are the focus of much of teaching and learning as we near the end of the century. As an example of each, let us begin with what we will call generative definitions. Define each of the following three words based on your own experiences.

critical:

> related to a process of questioning assumptions, going beyond traditional responses, taking a careful, thoughtful look, looking at something from a fresh or new perspective

pedagogy:

> *the how of teaching or instruction*

critical pedagogy:

> *the process of thinking and reflecting about how to teach and learn*

Now that you have mused and written your definitions, let me share with you some definitions that came from students who have finished their undergraduate work and are just ready to begin a teaching credential program. This was a highly diverse group that had not previously studied critical pedagogy. Together they had discussed and read about the idea for only a couple of days. Their definitions of critical pedagogy follow:

- a state of mind, a place of reference;
- a framework from which to build;
- a questioning frame of mind;
- it makes us double-check our action and the action of others;
- it makes me do the best I can;
- it empowers with a perspective needed to ask good questions; it makes me actively commit to do something;
- it makes me see beyond what was taught yesterday.

Now that you know how I feel about definitions, you will appreciate my trepidation in defining critical pedagogy. I am fearful to give a definition, but I know very well that my readers want one. In an earlier draft of this document, I attempted to solve this problem by hiding the definitions within paragraphs about teachers and learners. Or, at least I thought I was hiding the definitions.

I was walking through the computer lab and happened to glance down at a paper that a student had beside her computer. I noticed that it was the earlier draft of this document. I slowed my pace and looked more carefully at the hard copy to the side of the computer. I noticed with glee and dismay (oh, those darned contradictions of education) that she had found and highlighted in bright yellow all of the definitions of critical pedagogy I had placed in various paragraphs.

> *"If I understand this correctly, you don't want to define it for us; rather, you want us to find meaning for it based on our lived experiences," she said.*
>
> *"Yes, that is exactly what I mean," I responded. "But, I noticed that you have found all the definitions I thought I had so cleverly hidden throughout the document. You have highlighted them, even though I thought I had woven them within the context so that each reader would eventually discover and generate his own understandings of this somewhat abstract concept."*
>
> *"Yes, I could tell you didn't want us to memorize your definitions. I could tell you were trying to hide them, but my understanding is that critical pedagogy means we have to look back at our own histories and generate new questions in order to find new answers based on our knowledges, and literacies, and cultures, right?"*
>
> *"Right," I replied.*

Phony, from the True

> *The group was busily solving problems in the third-grade class. The teacher had written on the board:*

Estimation	Actual	Difference

> *First, the teacher asked the students to estimate how many rocks were in the piles on the table.*
>
> *"Lots."*

"37."

"83."

The children began to guess noisily and happily. When each group decided on their guess, they recorded their numbers on their individual papers and on a chart under the word estimation *on the chalkboard.*

Second, the teacher asked each group to count the actual number of rocks. They began counting each little rock and again recorded their numbers on their papers and on the chart under the word actual. *Many squeals of glee could be heard as the students discovered how many were actually in the pile. The problem of the day was to discover the* difference. *I noticed that the teacher did not use the word* subtract; *she only talked about finding the* difference.

The students began to talk and think; they soon discovered that talking and thinking were more difficult than guessing and counting. One particular group of four students was noticeably struggling. They debated counting and guessing and adding while all the time shoving their little pile of rocks around the table. However, no matter what they tried, they could not agree on the difference, *nor even how to find it. It seemed that the word* difference, *and not the process of subtraction, was the stumbling block. It appeared to me that they knew the concept of subtraction, but the word* difference *stumped them. Eventually, they returned to a discussion of* estimation *and* actual, *concepts that they knew that they knew.*

Suddenly, a little African American boy in this group shouted, "I get it! I get it! Let's just take the phony *from the* true, *and we will have it."*

His teammates immediately understood and successfully solved the problem through subtraction.

In this particular situation, the students knew the concept, but it was the language that was denying them access to the answer. In order to subtract, a concept they already knew, they had to find language that they understood. In addition, when they returned to their discussion of *estimation* and *actual* in order to find the *difference*, they were looking for some previous knowledge to connect with the new knowledge.

The same can be said for the language of critical pedagogy. Sometimes, when we bump into new language, it feels like we are being denied access to the concepts. Or, at least, that is how I felt when I first started reading the language of critical pedagogy. Many teachers and learners have lived the concepts of critical pedagogy; they know what it is; they just don't know that they know.

Finding the Phony.   We often would like to take the *phony* from the *true*. But, is there ever *one* truth? *one* answer? *one* way of knowing? *one* right way? I doubt it. And, certainly not in critical pedagogy. In this chapter, I will share the *truth* of critical pedagogy as I have experienced it. I hope that my *truth* is an authentic story that reflects my life in schools. I encourage you to reflect on my experiences, to muse on my musings, to think about my thoughts. However, my intention is *not* to transmit my knowledge as if it were the *one true* knowledge. Together, we will visit and revisit the concepts and language through the filter of real teachers and real students in real classrooms. The theory will be grounded in daily classroom practices so that you, the reader, can discover, generate, create, and internalize your own definitions.

LANGUAGE OF POSSIBILITY—LANGUAGE OF CRITIQUE

It is a common experience for educators initially to become aware of critical pedagogy through the unique language that surrounds it. This language is disquieting; we don't feel at home with new language. When we don't understand language, we are denied access to ideas, to concepts, to thoughts, to people. Where in the world did the language of critical pedagogy come from? Perhaps, the following conversation between twin six-year-old boys and their mom as they drove in the car will shed some light.

NICOLÁS: Who made up words?

MOM: What do you mean?

NICOLÁS: Who made the words in the whole wide world? Words like trees and bees?

MOM: How do you think words got made?

NICOLÁS: I don't know.

MICAEL, FROM THE BACK SEAT: White people. White people made them.

NICOLÁS: No, God made them.

MICAEL: White people.

NICOLÁS: God.

[*They begin to shout at each other.*]

MICAEL: White people.

NICOLÁS: God . . . God was here before people.

MOM: I think people invent words as they need them. (Smith, 1995, p. 250)

It's true, critical pedagogs talk funny; at least, some do, sometimes. Buzz words and jargon. We, in education, are often accused of this. I am personally not attracted to jargon, even though I have been accused of using it. Ouch. I remember a powerful voice (J. Stansell, personal communication, March 20, 1991) saying, "Joan, say what you mean, and mean what you say." It seems that this is my goal in this book. I am fully aware of the dangers I face in fulfilling my goal. In trying to simplify, I cannot slip into simplistic. I want to clarify, not trivialize. I want to expand the language, not reduce it. What do all of those words mean? When I started reading about critical pedagogy I felt that others knew, and I didn't. I felt as if I had less value, less status, and less knowledge.

The irony is that this new language helped me break out of previous ways of knowing. Another contradiction! The thing I thought was the barrier (language) was the very thing that helped me break through the barrier. The language of critical pedagogy made me quite crazy at first, and ironically, finally opened the door to more complex understandings for me. The language of impossibility became the language of possibility for me. The gate became the drawbridge. It helped me approach the other, on the others' terms; and not on my presupposed image of the other; or what I wanted the other to be. My wish is that when you have finished this book, you will feel at home with the language and ideas of critical pedagogy. Recently, Kitty, a teacher, expressed it this way.

Now that I am studying more and more, I have words that describe my beliefs. Before, I thought they were only mine. Now, I am finding that my beliefs are written about *in books.*

VYGOTSKY: REACHING BACK
TO MOVE FORWARD

In the process of teaching and learning I, like all of you, encountered many new ideas. Sometimes these ideas fit with what we have long intuitively felt, but never had the language or courage to express. I struggled to consume this new knowledge. As with Jonathan, I tried everything I philosophically believed in and didn't believe in. The more I learned, and the more I read, the more questions I had. It was a constant process, challenging all of my previously held assumptions of unlearning.

Finally, in desperation, I decided to try what I had always taught my students: Hook it onto prior knowledge. Construct meaning based on your own knowledge and experiences. My internal dialogue went something like this:

"What do I know?" I asked myself.
"Well, I know a little about language. Okay, that is a good starting point. Now, what language person, in particular, might be helpful?"
"Oh, yes, my old friend, Vygotsky." I answered myself.

I sat down with my worn and tattered *Thought and Language* (1962). I started to read and reread. I tried to connect thought with language; ideas with words. Vygotsky taught me again that if I had one little thought and one word, I could begin to generate meaning between the two. The words would multiply, and the thoughts would grow. The dynamic relationship between the two would continue to create new meanings.

This is exactly what I did in the early stages of my studying critical pedagogy. First, I grabbed any word of critical pedagogy; just one word. "Anyone can learn one word," I told myself. And, as the words grew, so did the thoughts, just as Vygotsky said they would (Wink, Putney, & Bravo-Lawrence, 1994, September/October).

In this case, language was the tool to help me understand. However, it did not feel like I was using a tool; rather, it felt like a process that enabled me to think more deeply and critically. A Polish friend told me about an English language class he had. He said, "They gave me this list of words, but didn't tell me what to do with them." Vygotsky helped me understand what to do with these new words of critical pedagogy; I had to hook them to thoughts.

The ideas of Vygotsky empowered my learning of the language and the thoughts of critical pedagogy. As I learned each new word and/or thought, new linkages would grow with my prior knowledge and existing experiential base. The most important lesson I learned from Vygotsky was that I had the ability to create new knowledge by using the relationship between thought and language.

Initially, I didn't even know the vocabulary; but, I knew that I knew the ideas. Kids in schools had long ago taught me these same concepts. My experiences had brought me to the same place. I just didn't have the language to express what I was feeling. So, in order to even start, I had to learn the words. And, as I learned the words (in context) and played with the words, they gradually became mine. The words were sinking into the region of thought. Language finally began moving toward thought. Initially, these words were symbols without meaning; I had to play with them, read them, write them, talk about them, and gradually meaning started to develop. But, the relationship between the words and the thought is never static; as words develop, thought develops; and as thought gradually develops, the words change with the emerging ideas. I only hope that Nicolás and Micael listened to their mom.

In my particular case, the language of critical pedagogy, which at first had alienated, infuriated, and exasperated me, finally empowered me. From Vygotsky, I have learned that our words matter. Our words are not just neutral squiggles on paper. They are not just neutral symbols. Our language joins with our thoughts to generate meaning. As we increase our use of words, our thoughts deepen. The language we use matters. Sometimes language hurts one group of kids, and sometimes it helps another group.

Critical pedagogy forces educators to look again at the fundamental issues of power and its relationship to the greater societal forces that affect schools — this comes dangerously close to being a definition! Critical pedagogy has made me look again at the fundamental issues of power that are involved in the creation of a "trash" track. Critical pedagogy is forcing me to think and rethink my lived experiences as compared with those of my African American colleague. "Critical pedagogy asks how and why knowledge gets constructed the way it does, and how and why some constructions of reality are legitimated and celebrated by the dominant culture while others clearly are not" (McLaren, 1989, p. 169). For me, critical pedagogy is a new lens that enables me to see more clearly my past, my present, and my future.

One of the frustrating aspects of the study of critical pedagogy is our tendency to want others to transmit their knowledge of what it means to us. *Just tell us what it means!* During my initial encounters with these concepts, I was exactly like this. I felt angry, alienated, and excluded from this new knowledge. Repeatedly, I went to my professors to implore them to "just explain it." They repeatedly handed me another book. Each book triggered more questions.

Eventually, I came to the realization that I would have to find meaning for myself based on my own lived experiences. I do not believe that I can transmit my generated knowledge to you; however, I can share my story and in the process you can make your own connections based on your knowledge and experiences. This is not the *Cliff Notes of Critical Pedagogy*, but it is a collection of understandings about the language of critical pedagogy.

CONSCIENTIZATION

The truth is that I can barely pronounce the word *conscientization*; not in English, not in Spanish, not in Portuguese. I understand it. I know when I didn't have it. (When I was in Benson, I had *Hooked on Books*; I did not have conscientization.) I know when I began to develop it. (After teaching and learning with those Benson kids for a decade.) I know when teachers and learners have it. (Once Jonathan broke through the barrier of decoding, he had it because he knew that he knew.) I know when students don't have it. I recognize it when it is emerging in learners. I respect it. I understand its power. I love it. I just can't pronounce it very well. Not only that, it is extremely difficult to explain to others. It took me about two years of reading hard books before I really got it. So, if after reading this section, you don't feel as if you understand it, it is okay. Patience is fundamental to our learning. Courage is fundamental to our learning. Just keep reading and reflecting and talking and writing; soon you will come to understand its meaning based on your experiences.

Conscientization moves us from the passivity of "yeah-but-we-can't-do-that" to the power of "we-gotta-do-the-best-we-can-where-we-are-with-what-we've-got." For example, I see teachers as powerful humans who can make a difference in the lives of students. However, they often feel weak because they see themselves as victims of a system that renders them passive. Conscientization enables students and teachers to have confidence in their own knowledge, ability, and experiences. Often people will say that conscientization is a power we have when we recognize we *know* that we *know*.

Another example I am presently living has to do with my single-eye contact lens. When I first received it, I was almost paralyzed with fear that I wouldn't be able to get it in; to get it out. Consequently, I wasn't able to do it. Once I knew that I knew (how to do it) I was infinitely more powerful. I no longer needed the doctor, the assistant, nor the box with instructions. I could depend on my own knowing. I know that I know. When it comes to putting in a contact, I am now empowered by my own knowledge of my power.

In schools and communities, conscientization is knowing we know, and it is more. It means that we have voice and the courage to question ourselves and the role we are playing in maintaining educational processes that we do not value. Recently, at a faculty retreat, I watched a colleague explain that she was teaching a concept she knows has been discredited by further research. We asked her why she continued to maintain a process she cannot support. She needs to know that she knows; she needs conscientization; she needs courage to stop maintaining processes she knows do not work. Later, at the same retreat, another colleague spoke about a test he gives his students every semester. I know him, and I know this test. It is everything he doesn't believe in. I asked him why. Why does he continue to give this test if it flies in the face of his considerable knowledge and experience? Later, when he was presenting to the entire faculty, he mentioned the test and said he just realized he didn't know why he was giving it. I predict he won't next semester. Conscientization is emerging. He is coming to know that he knows. He is finding the power of his own voice, his own knowledge, his own experiences.

When I think of conscientization, I never think of a definition. I always think of people. Let me tell you a story of two teachers: One has conscientization and the other doesn't, well, didn't.

Carmen Has It

I first met Carmen when she came to teach at a very low status, bilingual school in the South. I never could figure out why the district called this school the bilingual school; there was nothing bilingual about it. The teachers spoke English; the kids spoke Spanish. The teachers used English curriculum; the kids understood Spanish curriculum. I guess it was called the bilingual program because the Latino children went to school there. Until I met Carmen.

Carmen looked like a teacher who would be found in a Norman Rockwell painting. She had moved beyond the middle of life and had long salt-and-pepper hair pulled loosely into a topknot; small tendrils fell around her face. She had a slight build; but, there was an air of strength and health about her. She looked very much like a woman who for many years had worked long hours and had eaten sparingly. Her clothes were a no-nonsense cotton that served her well in the classroom; her shoes were sturdy, as was her character. More than anything, one immediately noticed a sense of peace and purpose. She was courageous and patient. This was a woman who had known many teachers, and many students, and many parents; together they had been reading the world, reading the word (Freire & Macedo, 1987).

Eventually, I came to learn many things about Carmen, and from Carmen. Carmen understood about learning, teaching, languages, literacies, cultures, knowledges. She had complex understandings and multiple perspectives. She thought kids needed to learn, so she taught in a language they understood: Spanish. In her class the students were continually generating language and ideas, language and ideas, language and ideas. I suspect she had read Vygotsky, too.

Carmen did not use the district-prescribed curriculum. She used the entire context of her students' lives for her curriculum. The state-mandated basals and materials served as just another resource to be used when needed. There were times when a certain activity viewed in isolation would appear to be much less than it actually was. Only the interaction of the entire context of her teaching could give full meaning to any activity.

For example, one day I walked into her class and noticed that Gilberto was, again, the center of attention. He was particularly adept at this, and I had come to think of him as Gilberto, the-most-frequent-office-visitor. Gilberto recently had a new, very short haircut. He, in true Gilberto style, had arranged all day for his peers to be more interested in his new haircut than the lessons the teachers had planned. Already that morning I had heard a lot of grumbling from other teachers about him. However, there was something different about the kind of attention he was receiving in this class. Carmen and Gilberto were hand-in-hand walking behind each student's chair so that each had an opportunity to touch Gilberto's head. As they walked, Carmen was teaching the words and ideas: brush, comb, shampoo, rinse, hot water, warm water, cool water. Gilberto sat down, and Carmen wrote their language on the board. Together they created new thoughts and sentences with their generated language. Carmen wrote everything on the board. Teodoro mentioned that his hair felt ticklish. Carmen wrote ticklish on the board, and the students read the word and giggled. Soon all the children had their own journals on their desks and were busy using their language to write new sentences. Carmen knew the importance of including the children and their world in her lessons. After this particular lesson, Carmen walked across the hall to Rainey's classroom.

Carmen knew the power of Gilberto and his new haircut; and, she *knew* that she *knew*: conscientization. And, she knew that Rainey, a beginning teacher, who worked with the same group of children for their English language development and their math and science, would need a little push in this direction, or she would have continued with her prescribed lesson on the colors in English. The children would have memorized those lists of words, but as the Polish student taught us: They wouldn't have known what to do with them. Carmen knew how to make those words and ideas work for her students. Carmen soon had Rainey and the students busily involved with funny new words in English — words like ticklish, prickly, spike, flattop — words that never would have been on the ESL list for memorizing.

Carmen and Gilberto had created an activity that mattered to the kids. Every minute was used for the learning and teaching process. In this classroom, Freire (cited in McLaren, 1989) would not find a "culture of silence." The children were not silent because they felt less or were afraid; they were silent only when it was meaningful in their learning. At the end of the day, each child had written a story, using all of their new words and ideas, about funny new haircuts.

Carmen, more than any other teacher, taught me the power of conscientization in the practice of her class. She knew her beliefs from years of experiences and books and ideas and people. She turned her beliefs into behaviors in every moment of her life. Her students grew to love themselves; their teachers grew to love the students; the students grew into their own biliteracy; and, the power of this pulled the community into the process. The peace and purpose that was Carmen transformed the students, her colleagues, and their students. As you read this book, please don't memorize a definition; just remember Carmen. In addition, reflect on someone you know who has conscientization, and please reflect on your own.

Conscientization is . . .

an awareness of knowing

courage to put the awareness/knowing into practice

The person I know who has conscientization is . . .

because . . .

In my own personal development of conscientization, I would say that I . . .

Rainey Doesn't; Well, Didn't

Rainey was as vivacious as Carmen was private. Rainey taught in English; Carmen taught in Spanish. Rainey had never been around Mexican kids; she continually complained to me about them and their behavior. Carmen had always been around Mexican kids; she continually told me how smart and loving they were. Rainey was new to teaching; Carmen was not. The first time I met Rainey in school, she desperately implored, "Okay, I've taught the weather in English — now, what do I do?" The first time I met Carmen, she matter-of-factly told me that I would need to get her some more books in a language the students could understand. It would be safe to say that Rainey did not have conscientization. Carmen did.

Rainey: BC. Let me describe some of Rainey's behaviors b*efore conscientization* and *before Carmen*. The following is a list of things she said about her students at the beginning of the year:

Ollie:	One of the worst.
Gilberto:	A terrible problem.
Carlos:	Ugh.
María and Irma:	Pitiful sisters.
Cristina:	Doesn't know anything.

The meetings with the families provided multiple opportunities to observe her behaviors, which told me much about her beliefs. Rainey would enter the school auditorium with a smile on her face, walk to the front row without speaking to any of the families, bury herself in the middle of the first row, where she was safely surrounded by the other teachers, and cross her arms. Several empty rows of auditorium seats always provided a safe buffer between the parents and the teachers. Rainey and many of her colleagues came from a tradition of family involvement that assumed teachers would talk; families would listen. The purpose of this approach to family involvement is to change the families. Rainey subscribed to this thinking. But that was BC.

Rainey: AC. Within a few short months, the power of Carmen began to work its magic. Rainey changed *after Carmen*. Rainey changed *after conscientization*. When she came to the family meetings, she would arrive with a smile on her face and walk up to all the families and use her limited Spanish. They warmed to her approach and were more than willing to teach her more. Her use of their language grew. Soon, she was visiting with so many family members as she entered the meetings that she could never make it to the safe front row of the auditorium. I began to find her in the middle of the parents wherever they were sitting. Rainey came to appreciate a new approach to family involvement. Instead of doing something to them, she came to understand why she should do things with them. Instead of trying to change the parents, she was soon trying to change the school.

Once, she and Carmen were discussing family involvement and what the families needed. Rainey suggested to Carmen that she could go to the university library and do a computer search to find out. Carmen nodded and added, "Or, we could ask the families." At the next family meeting, the teachers asked, and the families told them their needs.

The Families' Needs

more family meetings
a written copy of the teacher's schedule
an understanding of the assigned homework
more time with their children
less time with TV

Rainey and Carmen chuckled during the meeting as they thought about Rainey going to the library, instead of just asking the parents.

Another example of Rainey: AC happened about the same time. The results of initiating and implementing a parent advisory committee are not often visible immediately, but they are worth the wait. Carmen always went to visit in the homes of her students. This was a very frightening thought for Rainey, and she resisted for months. Finally, she went to visit in the home of Carlos, one of her students who previously had almost convinced her to leave the teaching profession because of his behavior.

One day I was walking down a corridor in this school and realized that I was looking at Rainey and Carlos as they leaned on their elbows and stared out the window toward the playground; their bodies made dark silhouettes against the sunlight. Their heads were about an inch apart, and they were both facing the playground. By the slow movement of their heads, I could see that they were quietly visiting. I quietly backed down the hall so as not to disturb them.

Rainey, BC, thought Carlos was the worst; she physically grimaced every time his name was mentioned. She and other teachers used to talk about him in the faculty lounge. I used to try to imagine how terrible it would be to be in the first grade, where all of those in authority were against me.

As I watched Rainey and Carlos talk quietly and stare out of the window, I remembered how she used to talk about him; now she was visiting with him. Rainey thought that Carlos had changed. I think that Rainey has changed.

I remember Rainey telling me about the home visit. She was astounded to discover that he had a good home environment, with a loving and supportive family; his brothers and sisters were successful in school. She was relieved to learn that Carlos's mom shared her concern for Carlos. The mother could not understand why Carlos wasn't learning at the same pace as his brothers and sisters. But, Carlos's mom was too uncomfortable and alienated to come to the school and discuss her concerns.

Rainey told me that before the visit, she assumed that Carlos' behavior was a result of his home. She assumed that the child, the child's family, and the child's culture were the principle causes of his failure. After the home visit, she began to work with his mom to understand his behaviors, and behavior immediately improved. Carlos is a different person when he is with Rainey.

However, Rainey still has a critical step to take. She still thinks that Carlos has changed. She needs to critically examine herself and her environment and come to the realization that she is a part of the process of transformation. In Carlos's search for knowledge and literacy, she is a significant variable. I like to think that if Paulo Freire had been with me in that hall, he would have told me that this was conscientization: a transformation of the learner as a result of interaction with the teacher.

However, I'm not worried about Rainey. If she can move this far towards an intercultural orientation in the time that I have known her, soon she will **know** that she **knows**, and she will go on to help others read the world and read the word (Freire & Macedo, 1987).

Rainy: BC

Before Carmen
Before Conscientization
Before Carlos

Rainy: AC

After Carmen
After Conscientization
After Carlos

CODIFICATION

Codification is the concept, captured on paper, in the dirt, on the chalk-board, on the wall. It is the thought, painted. It is the symbol, symbolized. I have known teachers to codify thoughts in pictures, in action, in clay, in paint. Before Paulo Freire was banished from Brazil for developing literacy among the native peoples, I always visualize him standing in the shade of a tree codifying with a stick in the dirt the powerful ideas of rage and oppression that the workers were expressing. I have no idea if he stood in the shade, and I have no idea if he ever used a stick to draw in the dirt, but this is the image I carry with me to make meaning of codification. I have to tell you that I think Freire was on to something with this idea of codification. It captures the best of many powerful approaches to teaching and learning. It brings in the students' world and builds knowledges and literacies based on their own unique experiences. It puts the power back into teaching and learning. And, it integrates the never-ending debate between *doing* and *living* critical pedagogy.

Remember Jonathan and his board, and the tongues, and the throats, and the tiny sounds: lip popper, lip tappers, etc.? Remember that I thought I didn't like it? Remember it opened the door for Jonathan? Could it be that it was a type of codification that was necessary for Jon's ways of knowing? For Jon, the concept was finally captured.

CULTURAL CAPITAL

Cultural capital refers to the behaviors, values, and practices that are valued by the dominant society.

Dawn worried that other teachers made disparaging remarks because her kindergarten students would not stand in a straight line. Although she was intuitively opposed to five-year-olds standing in a

straight line, she could see their failure to do so was having a
negative effect on her students. When she said "formense" they would
gather in a circle around her, arms around each other, look at her,
and smile. She thought that it looked like a group hug. The other
teachers thought that it looked like unruly, poorly behaved Mexican
kids.

She decided to teach them to stand in line so they could have
cultural capital. She told them to get in line and put their hands on
the shoulders of the person in front of each of them. They dissolved
into giggles as they tried to choke and to tickle each other. She took
them to the basketball court and told them to walk on the line where
they tiptoed as if on a high wire. In the classroom they lined up
sticks, rocks, blocks, pencils, and papers. Finally, they went outside
to wait for the buses. "Formense," she said. They immediately formed
the best straight line. The other teachers began to smile approv-
ingly.

When Dawn was in kindergarten, she had lots of cultural
capital. She knew what was socially and culturally expected in the
environment of school. She knew how to get into line, to keep her
hands to herself, and to be quiet at certain times. She didn't always
do it, but she knew. Now, as a teacher, Dawn discovered that her
students had little cultural capital, and they were blamed for it.
Dawn still struggles with this because she prefers the group hug.

Cultural capital is a process of powerful practices: ways of behaving, talking, acting, thinking, moving, etc. These practices are determined unconsciously by the dominant culture and are used to promote success for specific groups in our society.

For example, in North American businesses and educational institutions, it is believed that we must speak in a very direct and concise manner in order to succeed. This manner of speaking is gender-specific and culturally laden; European American men like to speak this way, and they like others to speak this way. These high-status speech patterns carry value and carry men to the top. This linear-speak is valued by the power structures in North America, but this is not true in much of the world. Many cultural groups find that it provides a limited context, and they prefer to speak in a more enriched contextual frame. Much of the world (including some North American women) prefer to tell stories to make a point; they prefer to provide many perspectives and variables because they believe listeners (readers) will generate meaning based on their own lived experiences.

Oftentimes the nondominant culture buys into this way of thinking; they support it and encourage it. For example, when women began moving into the upper ranks of business, some women wore business suits that looked very much like men's business suits. Some women tried to *look like* men so they could move ahead professionally. More recently, women seem to feel more free to dress like women. However, sometimes women still support more subtle forms of cultural capital. Their business suits may be gone, but often their linear-speak is still bouncing around the offices. I recently had a very bright young businesswoman tell me that "you have to talk like men in order to get ahead." I am confident that there are many powerful and effective ways of speaking. The dominant society uses cultural capital to lure the nondominant groups into being like them. Nondominant people often are recruited for diversity, and then powerful dominant forces try to change their ways of knowing and being.

Sometimes cultural capital varies from region to region. It changes in various parts of the country. I remember an 80+-year-old man, Mr. Tom, talking to me about his brother. Mr. Tom lived on a ranch on the prairies and placed much value on all that ranchers know about cattle. His brother had recently retired from a brilliant career as a Boeing engineer, but Mr. Tom dismissed his knowledge with one concise statement, "He doesn't know a damn thing about cows."

DIALECTIC

A dialectic is the tension of *yining and yanging* (the backing and forthing) of thoughts, ideas, values, beliefs. A dialectic is occurring as I write this chapter on definitions. I know readers feel *just-tell-me-what-it-means*, and I am feeling *just-discover-what-it-means*. This is a dialectic. I know that definitions can be very helpful along the unlearning curve, but I am terrified that someone will take them and memorize them. Please, please, please don't memorize these definitions. Please, please, please don't fall into the jargon pit. Definitions have value only if the reader sits, reads, reflects, connects, and muses on them.

A dialectic is what happens when you are sitting in a class, a presentation, an inservice. You have been talked at, talked at, and talked at. You can barely sit still because you have a different perspective; you understand in a totally other way. You want to jump up and share your thoughts and hear the thoughts of those sitting near you. Suddenly the presenter stops and asks the participants to discuss in small groups. The "backing-and-forthing" of ideas breaks out in each small group. This is good.

Paulo Freire talks about the dialectic of being "patiently impatient" (cited in Gadotti, 1994, p. 47). A dialectic involves seeing and articulating contradictions; it is the process of learning from the oppositional view. Jonathan has provided a dialectical learning experience for me. A dialectic brings to light a more comprehensive understanding of the multiple facets of "the opposite." As we learn while teaching, and teach while learning, we are in a dialectical process. Other dialectics mentioned in this book are:

> *courage and patience*
> *a caring heart and a critical eye*

DIALOGUE

Dialogue is change-agent chatter. Dialogue is talk that changes us or our context. Dialogue is profound, wise, insightful conversation. Dialogue is two-way, interactive visiting. Dialogue involves periods of lots of noise as people share and lots of silence as people muse. Dialogue is communication that creates and recreates multiple understandings. It moves its participants along the learning curve to that uncomfortable place of relearning and unlearning. It can move people to wonderful new levels of knowledge; it can transform relations; it can change things.

We visit with someone, and our world changes for the better. For example, a high status, wealthy woman in a local community has been writing letters to the editor of the local newspaper, speaking to the school board, speaking to administrators, and circulating a petition. Her cause is to redo the reading and language arts program in the local schools. I have questions like, "How much does she really know about languages? literacies? cultures? knowledges?" However, I have been so busy working on this book and trying to stay ahead of my students that I haven't done what I should have. I haven't called her to hear what she has to say; I haven't dialogued with her.

One of my friends, though, who is a teacher in the local schools, did make time to call and enter into a little change-agent chatter. As you will see (Figure 2.1), the dialogue of the two women demonstrates that they are generating knowledge and coming to understand together. They are discovering meaning as they visit. Their talk matters and will eventually have a significant effect on many students. The two women have known each other for

Dear Sally,

I received your letter yesterday. I must tell you how respectful I am of the courage this entire procedure has shown you to have. You should <u>never</u> be regretful for voicing a concern and taking action on that belief. That takes courage. I never saw the petition, so I don't know what it says. I heard there was a concern from you. Our shared past history told me that you weren't a hurtful or vengeful person. If you had a concern, it had to be well thought-out. I called because I was interested in your opinion. I still am. As you pointed out, people working and talking together can create change and more understanding between opposite philosophies. Sally, you opened the door. We need to make sure that the opportunity for dialogue does not close. I talked with the district personnel about some more public forums for parents to discuss concerns. You were/are exactly right about dialogue.

I would like to invite you to a small group of professionals who meet monthly. We get together to discuss holistic teaching and learning, read books and discuss them, and generally support one another.

The more I learn about education, the more I understand that I have much to learn. As a late starter, it is my job and my avocation. I love what I do. New ideas cause me great excitement. For many teachers, however, I suspect that this type of joy is gone. For me, change is acceptable and challenging. With our body of knowledge expanding daily, life is not going to be the same as 10 years ago. And, 10 years from now may be unrecognizable in terms of education. Alvin Toffler, the futurist says,

> The illiterate of the future are not those who can't read and
> write but those who cannot learn, unlearn, and relearn.

You can see why I believe in dialogue. Without it, learning, unlearning, and re-learning won't happen. Change is scary. The unlearn/relearn process is new ground. Whenever we change our minds about something, we are involved in the unlearn/relearn at some point along the continuum. I think that anyone on that continuum is exhibiting courage. Your courage to change is an example. I hope we can continue to dialogue.

Sincerely,

Donna

FIGURE 2.1   Sample letter arising from dialogue

many years; their children were in pre-K programs together. These two women have shared experiences. After their dialogue, they wrote letters to each other. I am including one of these letters as a sample of the dynamic nature of dialogue (see Figure 2.1). This letter, which was written by my teacher friend, was a followup to their initial dialogue. After they had spoken with each other, and written letters to each other, the first woman withdrew her petition and acknowledged that she had acted with misinformation. I will be watching this situation closely, as I suspect this ongoing dialogue will have wider ramifications for children. When she and my teacher friend join together there is a great potential for powerful change.

DISCOURSE

Remember when discourse was . . . well, what in the world was it?

Perhaps we remember discourse as something that was studied with rhetoric in college? Something more serious and more important than a discussion? Interaction? Something that carried status and power and was somehow related to profound speeches?

It turns out that discourse is not just the use of words. Rather, it is the use of loaded words that establish who is on which rung of the ladder. And, it turns out that there are lots of ladders, or discourses. Discourses reflect a certain place; they are all socially-culturally grounded. For example, I am not at home with the discourse of statistics; I can do it and talk it and think it, but, the truth is, I am just not at home with that particular discourse. In fact, when I find myself in that place, I have been known to invent language to make meaning of that context. I have a friend Debe who thrives on the discourse of statistics; I think she talks funny, and she thinks I talk funny in that environment. We both see and know in very different ways when it comes to the discourse of statistics. She is central to a group of my friends who love statistics; I am "the other." On that ladder she is several rungs above me.

Today discourse can sound like dialogue, only in discourse, the words carry subtle (and not so subtle) messages about power. It seeks to establish the hidden rules for who speaks and who listens; what knowledge is good and bad; whose words have more power and whose words are marginalized.

As I reflect back 30 years ago, it seems that the meaning has changed. Yet, another change. I remember my first conscious experience with discourse. I don't remember what it meant. But, I remember the professor who taught the class; I remember his name, his class, his walk, his eyes. I remember the fear we felt in the class. I remember reading, and reading and writing, and having to enter into discourse in the class. I remember how passionately he felt about discourse; it mattered to him. As the semester and nervous stomach aches continued, I remember I began to feel more confident; more important, (dare I say it?) more elite. I had status and privilege. I think the word *discourse* for him was more in line with rhetoric, and even, oratory. As I reflect on the unspoken feelings of that class, I can now see that even then the messages we received were filled with messages of power and lack of power. Through this vehicle of the discourse class, we were assigned status, power, and prestige. I was rewarded for my conformity with an A. I hope the meaning of discourse has changed!

To label any student *limited* is to limit how that student is institutionally perceived; how that student feels about her capabilities and potential; how peers feel about that student. But, to articulate the various levels of limitedness is to socially sort students' status, as can been seen in the following class filled with teachers.

> *The graduate class had several discussions about the hidden language we all use to produce and reproduce social status and power. We had focused on words such as LEP [limited English proficient], LES [limited English speaker], GATE [Gifted and Talented Education], challenged, disadvantaged, at risk, minority, etc. We had recently learned of a school with a program for "potential dropouts." After much discussion, we had agreed that to place a student in this program would send a negative message regarding our expectations for the student. The class had dialogued about the importance of critically reflecting on our own language; therefore, we were all a little surprised at the following discourse, which unexpectedly emerged in class.*
>
> *We were discussing how assessment of bilingual children often does not lead to programs that serve the needs of these students.*

"But, in our school we even have two levels of ESL instruction. One section is for the high-limiteds, and the other class is for the low-limiteds," a graduate student proudly told us. "I teach the low-limiteds."

Silence hung in the room, as we internalized the meaning of discourse.

Recently, a conversation with a friend/colleague provided an unexpected opportunity to reflect and act on the importance of discourse. As professionals, our language does make a difference, as seen in the following conversation. My colleague and I had been discussing the evaluation of a third colleague whose annual evaluation had not been successful.

JOAN: Do the written evaluations indicate that he has had any successful experiences with students?

T: Oh, yes, he does okay with *normal* students.

JOAN: With *normal* students? Who would that be?

T: Well, okay, I mean with *regular* students?

JOAN: With *regular* students?! And, who would that be?

T: Well, okay, what word do you want me to use?

JOAN: I don't know. Use an adjective. Who are you talking about?

T: Okay, I mean with Anglo, English-only students.

My colleague recognized the power of language. By labeling one group *normal* and *regular*, other groups in our program immediately were marginalized. This is how the norm is normalized, the regular is regularized, the standard is standardized. And, for professors to use this type of discourse, no matter how unintentional, is to lower the value of one group of students and to raise the value of another.

This point was recognized by another teacher in the area in a story that she shared.

I was visiting with another teacher who wanted to know why students who come from other countries often cross their 7's with a bar in the middle. I explained that they were clarifying the difference between a number 7 and a number 1. She nodded her head in understanding. She then wondered why they use a front tail on the number 1. I answered that it was to clarify the difference between a number 1 and a printed small letter l. She realized that some of her students did confuse the number 1 and the small letter l because of the North American style of writing. However, she ended our discussion with, "Why can't they just do it the normal *way?"*

Joining the Prairie Club

My family, friends, and I have been spending quite of bit of time on our ranch on the plains lately. This has provided many opportunities to think about being admitted to the discourse of the prairies. We immediately know when we are admitted membership and when we are denied membership. Dean, my husband, is gaining entrance into the Prairie Club because he looks like the other members of the club. He wears the same clothes, knows about cows, and has the same one-finger wave as he passes lonely trucks on the highway. He is hardier than the average, friendlier than the average, and taller than the average. When he speaks with the Prairie Club members, he uses the same quiet, reserved language that establishes credibility and respect. Slowly, the doors of the Prairie Club are swinging open, and he is being granted admission. The Club will affect him, and he will affect the Club.

Recently, California friends came to visit on the ranch in January. Never mind that they are the antithesis of every California stereotype, it was clear that the locals resisted allowing them to join the discourse of the rural and isolated plains. I noticed that my neighbors, with a twinkle in their eye, would periodically ask how our California friends were enjoying the Midwestern winter. It was clear that the hardy plains natives assumed that the California couple were suffering, which, in addition, provided a little entertainment for the charter members of the Prairie Club. Our California friends always responded simply and positively to questions about the cold weather, but it remained obvious that the Club members were reserving discourse membership for only the natives.

On one particular day, it was 0 degrees and the wind was blowing. The windchill was probably 30 below, and the howl of the wind created a forlorn sound across the prairies. My friend Sharon went with us in the cattle truck to feed the cows. En route to feed, we stopped to visit with some neighbors in the small grocery store/post office, which is the heart and soul of the Prairie Club. As Sharon blew through the front door, all eyes were on her. The store owner said what the others were thinking:

> *"Well, what do you think of this weather?"*
>
> *"Sure is* crisp*," Sharon calmly responded, slowly drawing out the sound of each consonant. A moment of silence hung in the air as the Prairie Club members stared at her and mused on how to handle this most acceptable, stoic, and understated response. Finally, the store owner, a high-status respected member of the ranch discourse community said,*
>
> *"Yes, you are right. It sure is* crisp*."*

With that brief discourse, Sharon was granted preliminary membership to this particular rural discourse community. Now, if she had said, "Whoa! It is *so* cold, I'm ready to return to the sunny coast," the door to membership in the discourse of ranches would have slammed shut permanently.

HEGEMONY

Hegemony is the domination of one group over another with the partial consent of the dominated group. It is the control of knowledge and literacy by the dominant group. In the following scene, a high school teacher shares with us how one type of cultural knowledge was affirmed and validated in her presence and another type of cultural knowledge was denigrated.

> *"Rap music and break dancing are not allowed at our school,"*
> *Mr. Smith, the principal, announced as he stormed into my class-*
> *room. He grabbed B.J. by the ear, literally pulling him out of the class.*
> *I was not physically strong enough to prevent him from dragging B.J.*
> *out of class and down the hall. I turned my attention back to the*
> *other students. After they were settled and working on their*
> *assignments, I walked down to Mr. Smith's office to check on B.J.*
> *"B.J. has been suspended. He has broken our rules. Perhaps this*
> *will set an example for the rest of the students that we set the rules,*
> *and when we do, we mean business," Mr. Smith told me. I just walked*
> *back to class shaking my head, but I couldn't help but reflect on the*
> *fact that Mr. Smith's (elevator) music was playing in the office of this*
> *school, which was located in the middle of the African American*
> *community in town.*

To be completely true to a definition of hegemony, B.J. would partially have to support Mr. Smith's action. We could say that B.J. began to reject rap music in favor of elevator music. The truth is, that didn't happen. However, B.J. did get very angry and is now considered a *problem* in school.

Enriched programs can be used as a hegemonic tool to groom one group and to marginalize and silence another. The following conversation, between a school secretary and a director of assessment, took place in the front office of an elementary school.

> *"This is a request for an assessment for the gifted program," the*
> *secretary said to the director.*
> *"Really? Who for?" the director of assessment responded.*

"José."

"A minority in Gifted? Those tests are in English. He doesn't know anything," the director said with a dismissing wave of her hand.

HIDDEN CURRICULUM

The hidden curriculum is the unexpressed perpetuation of dominant culture through institutional processes. The hidden curriculum is covert and insidious, and only a critical lens will bring it into view. It teaches what is assumed to be important. It defines the standard for the dominant culture. Critical pedagogy asks: Whose standard? Whose culture? Whose knowledge? Whose history? Whose language? Whose perspective? Critical pedagogy seeks to make pluralism plural: standards, cultures, knowledges, histories, languages, perspectives. Society has a tendency to domesticate students into believing the dominant view. Sometimes, it is supported by those who are marginalized by the hidden processes because (1) they haven't taken time to reflect critically on themselves and their roles, or (2) it is seen, cynically, as the superhighway that must be used to get ahead.

Sometimes, the hidden curriculum becomes such a part of the curriculum that no one notices it. For example, Vicky teaches in the Northwest. She is located in a very rural area that has a history populated by Native Americans, their culture, their language, and their ways of knowing. When she started teaching the junior high students, she noticed that the history of the local Native Americans was never studied, nor mentioned. The week before Thanksgiving, she asked a Native American eighth-grade boy what Thanksgiving was all about, and his response was: "The white man taught the savages how to plant." The room, filled with European Americans and Native American students, nodded in agreement. Only Vicky, the teacher, realized the devastating nature of the hidden curriculum.

The hidden curriculum can been seen in schools when little boys are called on more than little girls; when only Eurocentric histories are taught; when teenage girls are socialized to believe that they are not good in math and sciences; when heroes, and not heroines, are taught; when counselors track nonwhites to classes that prepare them to serve.

LITERACIES

Remember when literacy was reading and writing? Remember when we thought it was simple? Turns out, we were wrong. Perhaps our traditional assumptions of literacy were, not only simple, but maybe even simplistic.

The world has changed. Schools have changed. Students have changed. Now, we are coming to know multiple types of literacies: functional (languages of the streets and of life); academic (languages of schools and universities); workplace (languages of our jobs); information (languages of technology); constructive (languages we construct with the printed word); emergent (languages constructed with the text before we are really decoding); cultural (language that reflects the perspective of one culture — guess which one); and critical (languages that take us deeper into more complex understandings of the word and the world); and, finally, *literacies* as a new type of literacy that provides a foundation reflective of multiple experiences. Literacies are reading, writing, and reflecting. Literacies help us make sense of our world and do something about it.

I should have known literacy would be more complex than my traditional assumptions. I have watched many students develop (and not develop) their literacies in multiple ways. Jonathan is just one of the kids who has forced me to expand my understandings of literacy to be far more inclusive of all types of literacies.

All these literate processes have one common characteristic: They all are derived from social practices. Literacies are socially constructed often with our friends, in specific contexts, for specific purposes. Literacies do not develop in isolation; rather, literate processes grow from families, from schools, from work, from cultures, from knowledges, from technologies, etc.

If the new and more complex meanings of literacies begin to slip away from you, go back to "Discourses" and start again. It is a very similar concept. Debe was one to frolic in and relish every level, every facet, every dimension, every implication of the literacies of statistics. On the other hand, my literacy in that world could never have been considered plural, it was barely singular, which reflects my tiny understanding of statistics. Do not be fooled into thinking that the term *literacies* is just specific vocabulary for one particular context. It is not. It is the underlying ways of knowing, thinking, and making complex meanings. Each of us brings our own world when learning to read the word and reread the world.

Reading the Word and the World

Yes, critical literacy is reading and writing, but it's much, much more. Critical literacy involves knowing, lots of knowing. It also involves seeing, lots of seeing. It enables us to read the social practices of the world all too clearly. Critical literacy can push us into the zone of all-this-learning-really-isn't-so-great. Critical literacy means that we understand how and why knowledge and power are constructed by whom. For whom.

***Reading the Word* means:**

to decode/encode those words;

to bring ourselves to those pages;

to make meaning of those pages as they relate to our experiences, our possibilities; our cultures; and our knowledges.

***Reading the World* means:**

to decode/encode the people around us;

to decode/encode the community that surrounds us;

to decode/encode the visible and invisible messages of the world.

Traditionally, literacy has been "Reading the Word" (to paraphrase Freire and Macedo's title), or decoding sounds and letters. Critical literacy is "Reading the World," or encoding the power structures and our role in these processes (Freire & Macedo, 1987). Critical literacy recognizes that reading does not take place in a vacuum; it includes the entire social, cultural, political, and historical context. In what follows, I introduce you to a variety of people who have sadly read the world.

Many five-year-olds do this before they ever enter school. From TV, their family, trips to the store, they understand power. They read who speaks and who listens, where, and when, and to whom.

> *Five-year-old, José and his family nervously entered the school for the first time. They found the office and entered to begin the enrollment process. The secretary greeted them in English and handed them a packet of papers, all of which were written only in English.*
>
> *"Fill out these papers, please," she said to José and his family. As they looked nervously at the papers, Jane, the secretary, walked from around the counter, took José by the hand and walked out in the hallway. En route to a kindergarten class, she was joined by two teachers.*
>
> *"Whose class will he be in?" one of them asked.*
>
> *"Put him in Special Ed. He's from Mexico; he doesn't know anything," the other replied.*
>
> *Defeated and with his head down, José entered the classroom.*

José cannot yet read the word, but he has read the world very clearly. José started school the same day as Carmen, his teacher. Together Carmen and José taught me many things, including the meaning of critical literacy.[1] It was not long before José was engaged actively in reading and learning with Carmen in her classroom.

Chris, a young African American man, remembers when he was five years old and he learned to read the world.

> *When I was in kindergarten, I used to love to play with my friend, Peggy. She was European American, and I was African but we had not yet discovered that it mattered. All we knew was that we loved to swing and slide during recess. She was my best friend. One day she ran up to me and said, "You're black." She slapped me across the face and ran away. I remember crying. Later when I went home, I told my Dad. I could tell that he was very sad when he taught me to read the world.*

Orate and Literate Communities

We, in North America, put much faith in literate communities. We place high status on literacy, or reading and writing. Status and prestige are not assigned to those who are *illiterate,* a word that carries heavy connotations of *less. Illiteracy* has become a loaded, value-laden concept that is used to deny access to power. For example, "They are illiterate" often means much more than just not being able to decode. However, this is not true in much of the world (Skutnabb-Kangas, 1993). Many people in the world carry their knowledge in their head and not on paper. Important people carry important knowledge in their heads. Instead of being literate communities, these are called orate communities.

Jonathan has lots of orate knowledge although he still struggles with those spelling tests. However, his computer spell-check makes that irrelevant. His orate knowledge is highly relevant. Another example is a mariachis guitar player I knew. He carried the entire history of the Mexican revolution in his head, and he could sing and play it. After taking lessons from him, I learned the difference between orate and literate communities. I now have boxes and boxes of Mexican music with all the verses that I have transcribed from the tapes I made of him singing. These boxes are dusty and in my garage. His orate knowledge is still in his head.

So much of our knowledge serves us better when we carry it in our heads, and not on paper. For example, when I am in the grocery store, at the dinner table, at a coffee lounge, and people ask me questions about education, or multilingual education, or critical literacy, they don't want me to get out my papers, my books, my transparencies and answer their questions. They just want me to tell them in plain language something that is understandable.

If you are a teacher, there is a fun way to learn about orate and literate communities with your students. Start your class by explaining that for today, the time will be spent doing a big review of all that has been learned.

Tell your students they will need a blank piece of paper. Watch carefully what students do; they will immediately begin looking for papers with notes, for books, for old journals — any place where the knowledge is contained. Tell them: No, no, no. Use your brain; just brains, no books, no notes, no charts, no index cards. Just brains. Just orate literacy. Begin your review with some leading questions of what has been studied. You and the students will learn together that much of our knowledge is not carried in our heads; it's in our books; we only access it. I suspect there is a lot we could learn from orate people who are often referred to as *illiterates*.

I was reminded of this again recently when I read a note a local teacher had written for me. She teaches in a junior college.

Sometimes a situation with a student arises that makes us question our fundamental beliefs, and sets us moving along the path of unlearning, then relearning. We assume, from our literate perspective, that reading and writing are essential. However, students who come from an oral language tradition have lived quite happily and successfully for years without reading or writing. When these students move from an orate to a literate culture, we assume they will follow a prescribed path to literacy: listening, speaking, reading, and writing in their new language. We base these assumptions on our own experience. I had the following conversation with an adult Hmong student.

SARAH: Ko, I'm curious about something. Can you tell me, now that you read and write English, do you write down the stories from your culture so you won't forget them?

KO: Well, no. We prefer to use video.

This conversation stuck in my mind for about a year, surfacing and resurfacing from time to time. If students tell us they have a preferred way of learning, or recording, shouldn't we utilize that information? For students from an oral language tradition, the path to literacy should perhaps be listening, speaking, making videos, reading and writing. I'm now researching this for my thesis. Thanks, Ko!

PRAXIS

These stories are my praxis. My theory and my practice have joined together in the creation of the stories in this book. The stories reflect practice in classrooms that is grounded in theory. The theory is to be discovered in the practice. The stories reflect how beliefs become behaviors in the classroom, and how we can reflect on our beliefs by critically examining our behaviors. I am one of those teachers who focused on only practice for many years. I didn't even realize that in those years of teaching, I was building theory. It was only after I went back to graduate school that I discovered, to my great joy, that there were books about what my students had been teaching me for years. To this day, I see my former students' faces when I read theory, talk about theory, reflect on theory. I came to theory through practice. Some do it the other way around.

Praxis is the constant reciprocity of our theory and our practice. Theory building and critical reflection inform our practice and our action, and our practice and action inform our theory building and critical reflection.

This semester I am teaching a methods course that is designed to assist English-dominant teachers who are working in a multilingual context. We focus on methods, on practice, and on the how-to, even though it is hard for me. After years of practicing practice, my bias is now on theory. The why is more interesting to me than the how. However, this is a methods course, and we practice various methods. One night in class, I slipped in a little why, and the students seemed very responsive. After class, a teacher was walking out and said to me, "A little theory never hurts." And, I thought, "Yes, and a little practice never hurts." That is what praxis is: practice grounded in theory and theory grounded in practice.

PROBLEM POSING

Problem posing is much more than just a method, or a series of methods. In chapter 4, I will offer various ways of initiating this theoretical construct in the classroom. My purpose here is to generate a definition or a description of problem posing, which is central to critically teaching and learning. Jonathan is an example of difficult problem posing for me. Problem posing brings interactive participation and critical inquiry into the existing curriculum, and expands it to reflect the curriculum of the students' lives. The learning is not just grounded in the prepared syllabus, the established, prescribed curriculum. Problem posing opens the door to ask questions and seek answers, not only of the visible curriculum, but also of the hidden curriculum. Problem posing is very interested in the hidden curriculum, which is why many are uncomfortable with it. Problem posing causes people to ask questions many do not want to hear. For example, in the following description of a family meeting, there is problem solving, which brings about a *feel-good* sensation, and there is problem posing, which causes some to feel uncomfortable. Both problem solving and problem posing are existing simultaneously with very different consequences. This family meeting took place in the school of Rainey and Carmen, whom you have previously met.

The problem to be solved was that parents had quit coming to the family meetings. Families felt alienated; teachers blamed them for not attending, and the state agency was asking why families weren't involved in the education of their children. The problem for the district was to get the families involved. They needed to solve this problem, or state funds would be cut. The school had a new principal who actively worked with Carmen, Rainey, and all the teachers to find ways to make the families feel more welcome and more involved. At this point, only Carmen was making visits to the students' homes. Soon, the principal started making visits with Carmen; and eventually, she felt confident enough with her limited Spanish to make the visits alone. The families, of course, responded very positively. Other teachers began to visit the homes, instead of sending messages home telling the parents to come to school. Soon, the teachers felt there was reason to believe that they could have a family meeting, and the families would come. The first meeting was scheduled. Invitations were sent to the families in their language; a door prize was offered; and the children were prepared to share during part of the meeting, which was scheduled to be held in the school auditorium.

The parents arrived and sat in the back rows. The teachers arrived and sat in the front row. Three empty rows of auditorium seats separated the parents and the teachers. The parents were welcomed by one of the teachers, and the children performed. A guest speaker from the state agency spoke to the families about the importance of their involvement in the education of their children.

Her presentation to the parents was articulate and forceful. She encouraged the parents to turn off the TV and talk with their children. She explained to the parents that what they teach at home is as valuable as what is taught in school. She followed this by talking about the transferal nature of language: What the kids know in Spanish, they will know in English, too. I could see the parents nodding their heads in agreement. She encouraged the parents to ask questions, and not just who, what, and where, but also, why.

The meeting lasted a little more than an hour. When it was over, the parents began to gather their tired children. Among the teachers in the first row there was general agreement that the meeting had been a success. They had solved their problem. The families came.

Why did I seem to be the only one who was disappointed? Very little meaningful interaction took place between the parents and the teachers. No one had asked the parents how they felt, what they needed, what their concerns were. The entire evening had been a monologue; the families had been talked at. I had hoped for a dialogue.

However, not all problems are so easily solved. Sometimes, problem posing spins off of problem solving. As the teachers were smiling among themselves, and the parents were beginning to gather their children, an older man, who looked more like a grandpa, stood up and faced the stage of the auditorium. Very seriously and respectfully, he asked all of those in the front of the auditorium:

"¿Por qué enseña a los niños en una lengua que no entienden, y entonces los retienen?" *he asked me.*
(Why do you teach our children in a language that they don't understand, and then flunk them?)

Silence hung in the room. No one answered him. Everyone silently left the auditorium. This is problem posing, as opposed to problem solving. The man had questioned the established processes, which were obviously failing. The children were not learning, and the state agency wanted to know why. So did this man. This was a real problem, based on his lived experiences, which mattered to his family. He posed the problem, and many in the room came to understand that it is easier to problem solve than to problem pose.

TO GROOM

It all seemed so simple when all we had to worry about was infinitives, passive voice, gerunds. I was groomed to be a teacher, a secretary, or a nurse. No one ever specifically said that to me, but I received the message in multiple ways; I read my world. Very early I understood that I could never be a secretary or a nurse, so that left just one choice. I really never questioned it. And, as I reflect on those who groomed me, I am sure they were not aware of it, or they were doing what they thought was right for the time. My brother was never groomed to be a teacher, a secretary, or a nurse.

Grooming is preparing one group for a high status place in life. Grooming is akin to putting one group on a superhighway and the other group on a rough and bumpy road. When the group on the highway arrives first, it is assumed that they got there because they deserved to, because they worked harder, because they are smarter. For my age group, it is particularly easy to understand grooming when we consider our own experiences. Little boys were groomed to be bosses; little girls were groomed to be secretaries. I think, as a society, we have developed more complex understandings of this process.

I literally had just written that sentence when an outraged Dawn, our daughter, called and read this article to me.

Despite three decades of affirmative action, "glass ceilings" still block women and minority groups from the top management ranks of American industry, a bipartisan federal commission said Wednesday in the government's first comprehensive study of barriers to promotion.

White men, while constituting about 43 percent of the work force, hold about 95 of every 100 senior management positions, defined as vice president and above, the report said.

The Glass Ceiling Commission, which spent three years studying the issues, noted that 97 percent of senior managers in Fortune 1000 industrial corporations are white males, and only 5 percent of the top managers at Fortune 2000 industrial and service companies are women, virtually all of them white. Two-thirds of the overall population and 57 percent of the work force are female or minority, or both. ("Glass ceiling intact," 1995)

I guess I was wrong about us developing more complex understandings about boys being groomed to be bosses and girls being groomed to be assistants. What a waste of talent; what a waste of resources when only a small part of the population is allowed into positions of authority. I do not believe that 95–97 percent of the men are smarter and more productive; I do believe that they were groomed for these positions by hidden institutional and societal processes that we have failed to recognize.

Grooming still exists in overt and covert ways. Race, class, and gender are variables that determine your path: the superhighway or the dirt road. Those of us who have bumped into the "glass ceiling" have a moral mandate not to let others behind us have the same experience. Have you ever visited Washington, D.C.? It is frightening to see the grooming of white people to rule and the grooming of brown people to serve. It is a tragic contradiction of life that, in the assumed center of democracy, it is so easy to see which race has been placed on the superhighway and which race has been placed on the bumpy, dirt road.

Sometimes, these processes of grooming are an inherent part of specific lesson designs. For example, in the following activity, who is being groomed?

Around the World

This is a great name for a not-so-great math activity. The overt objective is for students to have an opportunity to practice a skill or to memorize a fact. The objective in this particular class was to review addition by using flash cards. The real objective was to win. This is what happened on the day that I watched this activity.

Rainey, the teacher, sat on a chair in front of the room; the children were seated at four groups of tables. Two children stood up, and Rainey held up a flash card with an addition problem. The child who said the correct answer first, as determined by Rainey, was the winner. Then that child would move on to compete with the next child. The loser sat down. I studied the individual faces as they won and lost; stood up and sat down. The winners received cheers and applause from their peers and moved on for more practice. The losers sat down and did not get to practice. Thus, the ones who needed less, received more; and the ones who needed more, received less.

Despite my apprehension about this, the activity appeared to be a resounding success. All the children were squealing with glee. The principal passed the door, and looked in with an approving look on his face. The lesson certainly appeared to be student centered and very interactive, not to mention fun! However, the primary focus of the activity was on the winning, not learning. Several students in particular caught my eye.

First, I noticed Irma, the cheerleader, who was a consistent loser. Each time someone said the numbers faster than she did, she had to sit down. She must be an amazingly resilient child because, each time after she sat down with a very dejected look on her face, she would quietly stare at the floor for about two minutes and then begin cheering wildly for the others again. I still do not know if Irma can add, but I'm not sure that it mattered in this activity.

The second child who caught my eye was Rosio, the loser who can add. Now, how could this happen? At the beginning of the game, I did not know Rosio, nor her math abilities, nor her level of fluency in English. But, I did notice that throughout the game, she was very quiet and still. When it came her turn to stand, she did so slowly and always was immediately forced to sit down because she didn't say anything. It appeared she could not add, but later I learned that she could add very well.

When the math activity ended, I asked Rainey if I could take Rosio to a little table and work with her. We began in Spanish, and

Rosio communicated very little with me. I asked if she knew English, and she said yes. I asked her if she wanted me to use English or Spanish; she immediately replied, "English." Rosio answered 80 percent of the addition problems correctly. When she had trouble, she would count the beans we had on the table, and then she had 100 percent accuracy. Why then didn't she win some of the rounds of competition? Rosio is a very quiet and shy girl. She thinks carefully before answering.

This activity was designed to reward those who think and speak quickly and loudly; it also grooms those who know, and eliminates those who need to know (Wink, 1991). Despite its great name, this activity benefits those who least need it. Those with the most, get the most. Those who need this type of structured practice stay in their seats. Sometimes these classroom activities are even more subtle, but just as deadly, because you have to be able to cut through sentimentality to understand the dynamics of power that are being constructed for one person or one group.

TO NAME

To name is to call an *ism* an *ism:* racism, classism, sexism. Naming is talking about the corruptible colonization, the damnable domination, the insidious supremacy that many marginalized groups have experienced, but have been conditioned not to mention. Naming is talking honestly and openly about one's experiences with power and without power. The A Team gets huffy when they hear the B Team name. The A Team responds with sentences that begin with "Yeahbut, ..."

Naming is more than just articulating a thought; it is more than just talking and labeling. Naming is when we articulate a thought that traditionally has not been discussed by the minority group, nor the majority group. Naming takes place when the nondominant group tells the dominant group exactly what the nondominant group thinks and feels about specific social practices. To name is to take apart the complex relationships of "more" and "less" between the two groups. For example, when little girls tell little boys (or when women tell men) that they hate the "glass ceiling," they are naming. When women say they hate it that men, 43 percent of the workforce, hold 95 percent of the senior managerial positions ("Glass Ceiling Intact," 1995), they are naming. And, when ethnic minorities say that they hate it that the remaining 5 percent of those managers are women, and only white women, they are naming. When African Americans say they hate it when blacks in the public-sector jobs earn 83.3 percent of the median income of whites (Bancroft, 1995), they are naming.

A friend, Verena, who lives in one of the northern states, wrote me a long letter about a school at which she had found a job. She had discovered terrible racist policies that were hurting the group of Native Americans and African Americans. As she desperately needed this job, she was upset about what to do. She wrote, "I have to make a choice to teach and play the game, or expose what is going on. If I do that, I am sure that I will eventually lose my job." If Verena decides to expose the racist policies, she will be "naming." And, if she doesn't, it will be because she has a fear of naming.

Earlier, I told you that I went to college and pretended I couldn't type because I didn't want to end up typing (as a secretary) for a man (as a boss). At that time I didn't have the language to articulate and name the gender-specific role that I could easily see had been assigned. And, even if I would have had the thought and the language to be able to talk about why women shouldn't type for bosses, I would never have done it. Even if I could have named, I would have been afraid to name. I still struggle with this. Courage and patience.

TO MARGINALIZE

To marginalize is to place someone or something on the fringes, on the margins of power. To be marginalized is to be made to feel less. Sometimes teachers marginalize specific groups of students. Remember when I told you about my colleague who labeled some students *normal* and *regular*? That is marginalizing. What group has been devalued in the following phone conversation?

TEACHER #1: Hi. This is Amy Jones. I understand that you are going to be my substitute tomorrow. I didn't leave any special plans. I want to tell you a little about my class and what you'll be doing tomorrow.

TEACHER #2: Great! I'm glad you called.

TEACHER #1: My room is way in the back of the school, Room 42. It's a sheltered English class. They are third, fourth, and fifth graders. Several languages are represented in this group.

TEACHER #2: Oh, I remember your class. I substituted in Room 43 yesterday, which is the special education class. I brought one of the students to your room so he could paint with your class. You may remember me.

TEACHER #1: Sure, I remember you. But listen, my kids are great. They are normal. They aren't stupid or crazy like "those" kids next door.

Certain trigger words often give you a hint that marginalizing is coming. Words like *normal*, *regular*, *those people*, and *them*. When you hear these, you can almost be assured that someone is going to be marginalized.

In the following statement that a teacher made to me during a staff development day, can you see which group has been marginalized?

TEACHER A: Give me one of those Asians with glasses any day before a Mexican!

TO SCHOOL

Schooling refers to the hidden educational processes by which schools impose the dominant ways of knowing on all. We have been schooled to think in traditional ways. One problem with that is that we now often have schools filled with traditional teachers and nontraditional students.

For example, I have mentioned to you that I was schooled to write in a traditional way; it was linear, dense, distant, neutral, and boring — none of which I am. I wrote in academicese; I hid behind my jargon. As I reflect on my old writing, I can see more and more of my male professors in every sentence. My old writing reflects them very well. My writing of today reflects me. It is everything I was schooled not to do: tell stories, be circular, be passionate, use real language. More than anything else, I was schooled to believe that I was writing for someone else; it had never entered my head to write for me, to write to make sense of my thoughts.

I must not be the only one who had this experience. My grad students initially think they are writing for a grade in the grade book; they want to know exactly what I want; they want to know how many pages. I just want them to write and make meaning of ideas that are bouncing around in their heads. I want them to write and to get smarter. I will respond as I come along for the cognitive ride. Who knows what we will learn, but we will learn. Recently, I was reading Sandy's journal. Sandy is a young grandmother who is back in college.

I have been *schooled* to believe that my thoughts did not matter. For example, I have been *schooled* to believe that I should not share a thought unless I could cite the authority. I am learning now that my thoughts matter. This is so new that it can be scary. Being asked to think for myself and then commit it to paper is a challenge: It flies in the face of everything I have ever been conditioned to do. Schooling is alive and well in me.

TO SILENCE

I am still silenced a lot. I struggle with silence. Men can silence me more than any other group. The old socialized patterns run so deeply that it is hard for me to break them even when I understand and can articulate the dynamic. When committee meetings get "hot and heavy," I still sink into silence. Breaking the old domesticated patterns of silence is still a struggle for me. However, now I *see* silencing. Previously, when I was silenced, I did not know it; I did not understand it; I did not recognize it. If fact, I bought into it and supported it with my behaviors. When I was silenced, I cooperated and perpetuated the process. Now, when I am silenced, I understand what is happening. Now, I can name it. However, I still struggle with my fear of naming. Sometimes, when I am in university committee meetings with many full professors, I am painfully aware that the insidious dynamic of silencing is controlling the agenda; I am painfully aware of my own fear of naming. The invisible agenda of who speaks and who listens often takes my mind from the visible agenda. I am always aware of the delicate balance between courage and patience as we move critically together toward a more democratic society. In my own context, I have noticed that (1) most full professors are men; (2) they are not aware that they are silencing others; (3) the few full professors who are women do not silence me. I know that this tells lots about my sociocultural context and about me. (I told you early in this book that I don't always like learning; for example, right now.) However, my experiences have taught me that this social dynamic of silencing plays out every day in all contexts. Sometimes we just don't see it. I guess my message is that we should *see silencing and stop silencing*.

I watch in amazement in my grad classes when certain students speak freely, but I am particularly aware of those who are still silenced. They feel as deeply; they know as much. I watch which individuals are silenced by others. I watch which groups are silenced by other groups and have noticed that silencing has a certain pattern:
Often,

- those who have more, silence those who have less;
- those who are from the dominant European American culture silence those from non–European American cultures;
- boys silence girls;
- men silence women.

Often,

- men don't know it;
- boys don't know it;

- European Americans don't know it, and
- those with more don't know it.

Silencing is usually a quiet and insidious process. Sometimes those who are being silenced know it, and sometimes they don't. Those who are doing the silencing rarely know it.

TO SOCIALIZE

Society sends many messages to each of us. Sometimes we hear those messages, and sometimes we don't. However, when we consciously or unconsciously accept those messages and live those messages, we are being socialized.

This took place in a fourth-grade classroom when the teacher announced the students would clean out their desks on Friday. Throughout the week, the students waited patiently for the Great Cleaning Day. When Friday finally came, papers and books and giggles filled the room — except for one boy, who did not take part. This boy comes from a culture that believes little boys do not clean; little girls and women clean. His mother came after school to clean his desk as this was work not befitting a young man.

This example is quite vivid and easy to see. Many times we do not recognize, see, nor understand the hidden socializing that is taking place. For example, from the point of view of this little boy and his mom, he is not being socialized; it is just the way things are. From the point of view of the teacher who told the story, it was an outrage. It is not really so different from the way I was socialized as a child. I cleaned; my brother did not.

Another example of socializing happened to us when we had an exchange student from Mexico. Laura was from Mexico City and came from a very enriched background that included ideas, books, laughter, love, and lots of money. Her family had many servants to make life easier. She left the urban confines of Mexico City and came to the desert ranch to live with us.

Suddenly, we realized that she had never done any of the indoor or outdoor chores that we had socialized Dawn and Bo to believe were part of everyone's responsibility. Washing and ironing clothes presented a particularly sensitive area. Bo and Dawn were in junior high and high school, respectively, and had been doing this for themselves for years. Dawn, as a grade-school feminist, was quick to make sure that if she did her own clothes, her little brother sure would do his. So, Bo grew up believing that if I washed his treasured T-shirts (a.k.a. rags) and jeans, they would be ruined with hot water or a hot drier. I socialized him to believe that only *he* could take care of *his* clothes. So, now suddenly, both of our kids were very eager to see if I would wash and iron *Laura's* clothes. They understood my vulnerable position as it related to justice and equity, and they relished every minute of my dilemma. After reflection, I realized that I couldn't undo all of my socializing of my own kids, and that Laura would have to learn to wash and iron her own clothes. I can still remember all three of the kids standing in the washroom while Bo and Dawn smugly taught Laura how to wash. Laura did all of her own washing; she never did iron, but then neither did Dawn and Bo. Laura is back in Mexico City now and no longer washes her own clothes. She is now socializing others to believe it is their job.

VOICE

Walk into any classroom, any teachers' lounge, any school office and see if you can tell who has voice. Who uses their voice to express their perspective? their view point? their way of knowing? Whose voice is promoted and valued? Whose voice is discredited with a wave of the hand? Courage is related to voice; it takes courage for some to express their voice. Voice is the use of language to paint a picture of one's reality, one's experiences, one's world. I am more interested in the voice that traditionally has not been heard.

The voice of those who traditionally have not been heard is usually embedded with varying degrees of resistance, rage, and a hint of resolve. I vividly recall, as a little girl, standing in a rural, isolated spot where the gas station/general store was the hub of the community for many, many miles. I remember the two outhouses behind the store: One had an old sign that said "Whites only" and the other had an old sign that said "Indians." I remember looking at the signs, and knowing something was terribly wrong, but I said nothing. I had no voice. I remember being asked to carry moldy bread onto the Sioux Indian reservation to the various families. I can still feel the shame I felt handing the bread to the women who answered their doors. But I would never have dreamed of expressing myself. I had no voice. My resistance, rage, and resolve were silenced. Most of my life has been dominated by the "voice" of one powerful group. This *monovoice* has been very limiting for many. As we near the end of the century, more and more voices are being heard. Multiple voices are moving us forward. The broader the diversity of voices, the greater the quality of society. Our society is becoming more vibrant, more enriched, and more exciting. It represents more of us. This traditional *monovoice* is transforming itself into a new *multivoice*, and not everyone is happy about it.

The following voice comes from Sheila, who is discovering hers as she prepares to be a teacher.

I wonder how much voice I will have when I'm teaching. I have recently left a career in management to become a teacher. During my years in management, I became one of the top employees where I worked: top in responsibility, not in authority. It seemed to me that the "voices" of women were not valued because the system was "just fine."

The majority of teachers are women, but their voices are just whispers. Women and minorities need to be at the top levels of school systems, and we need more men at the elementary teaching level.

Cummins said, "Unless we ourselves are empowered, we cannot be involved with any other processes of empowerment. To be voiceless is to be powerless. If we view ourselves as helpless, we are" (Cummins, 1989). I thought that it must be easy for him to say. He is a man, not teaching in the elementary school with someone else holding his future in the palm of their hands. Critical pedagogy has helped me to understand what teaching should be about— encouraging teachers to be professionals.

As Sheila is discovering her voice, she is "voicing" one of the most difficult questions of the study of critical pedagogy: Why so few women? Why so many men? Critical pedagogy has caused me to reflect seriously on the moral mandate that falls to those of us (women and minorities) who have survived a career of trying to change the system. My experience teaches me that many women see and know in critical ways and are moving to voice. I note with interest that we are in good company when we move into relearning and unlearning. In a dialogue, Donaldo Macedo is asking Paulo Freire how he would respond to his omission of the voice of women in his earlier works. Freire responds by saying, "I believe that the question feminists in the United States raise concerning my treatment of gender in *Pedagogy of the Oppressed* is not only valid but very timely" (Macedo, 1994, p. 106).

The purpose of this chapter has been to focus on one central question: What in the world is critical pedagogy? My intention has been for you to discover meaning based on your own experiences and knowledges. My purpose has not been to provide a list of definitions for you. However, on the very day in which I was finishing this chapter, I found the following paper among a large stack of graduate students' work on my desk. This piece of paper was from a student and was entitled *Scribble Notes*. The first paragraph seemed like a powerful definition of critical pedagogy for those who would like to have it. As I say, sometimes these definitions just fall from heaven. Lily, a teacher, wrote:

Critical pedagogy is a process of learning and relearning. It entails a sometimes painful reexamination of old practices and established beliefs of educational institutions and behaviors. Critical pedagogy causes one to make inquiries about equality and justice. Sometimes these inequalities are subtle and covert. The process requires courage and patience. Courage promotes change and democracy provides all learners equal access to power.

What in the world is critical pedagogy? It is certainly more than is written in this chapter, and it is as much as we allow it to be in our own ways, in our own communities. Critical pedagogy is more than the sum of its parts; it is more than a list of definitions of the words that have come to be associated with it. Lily, wisely, did not fall into the trap of seeing only the separate words of critical pedagogy. She put it together holistically after much reading and reflection. She made meaning of all the parts based on her experiences in life and in schools. Critical pedagogy is a process that enables teachers and learners to join together in asking fundamental questions about knowledge, justice, and equity in their own classroom, school, family, and community.

> *Beatriz visited a designated bilingual classroom in the school where she teaches. As she entered, she noticed the room was physically divided by the strategic placement of the desks, which divided the room in half. The English-speaking students were on one side of the room, and the Spanish-speaking students were on the opposite side. When the students began reading, the Spanish-dominant students read in a Spanish basal with the aide. The teacher worked only with the English-dominant students and chose themes from the core literature, which was in English. The thematic unit and core literature were totally unrelated to what the Spanish-dominant children were reading.*

Beatriz told us that before her study of critical pedagogy, she would have thought this was a good bilingual classroom because the Spanish-dominant children were using their primary language. However, now she understands the perpetuated inequity, which is done, in this particular instance, under the guise of bilingual education in this classroom. Critical pedagogy is a lens that empowers us to see and to know in new ways. When we last spoke with Beatriz, she had begun a dialogue with her colleague in this classroom. Critical pedagogy leads us from silence to voice.

In this chapter, the language of critical pedagogy has been seen in real classroom experiences with the hope that it will help readers to generate and expand their own meanings for critical pedagogy. In the next chapter, I will examine the question: Where in the world did it come from? Before moving on, are there other words and ideas of critical pedagogy that are meaningful for you? Language is never static; it continues to grow and change.

LOOKING AHEAD FOR YOUR THOUGHTS AND LANGUAGE ON CRITICAL PEDAGOGY

What are your own words and ideas?

NOTE

1. Critical Literacies. If you are intrigued with this concept, I strongly recommend that you read *Critical literacy: Politics, praxis, and the postmodern* (1993) by Colin Lankshear and Peter McLaren, published by SUNY at Albany, New York; *Literacies of power* (1994) by Donaldo Macedo, Westview Press, Boulder, Colorado; *Literacy: Reading the word and the world* (1987) by Paulo Freire and Donaldo Macedo published by Bergin and Garvey of South Hadley, Massachusetts; and *With literacy and justice for all: Rethinking the social in language and education* (1991) by Carole Edelsky, published by Falmer Press of Bristol, Pennsylvania. The topic of critical literacies is just too deep and too wide for the confines of this little book.

chapter 3

Critical Pedagogy

Where in the World Did It Come From?

Throughout this text, I hope to make critical pedagogy more meaningful for teachers and learners by sharing four central questions about critical pedagogy: What is it? Where did it come from? How do we do it? And, why does it matter? The spirit of inquiry that is fundamental to critical pedagogy has caused me to seek answers for these questions. In the previous chapter, I wrote about the big ideas in critical pedagogy: What in the world is it? In this chapter, we will follow the roots of critical pedagogy from the Latin Voice, to the European Voice, and finally to the multiple voices of North America. I realize that when I begin to speak of the critical voices of North America, I will inevitably omit someone. Therefore, in this chapter I will direct my comments to the critical theorists who have most directly influenced my own experiences and thinking during the last few years. My purpose is to tell the big story that lies behind those big words and ideas. The historical roots of critical pedagogy, as seen in Figure 3.1 on page 64, spread to many parts of the world. As I paint this picture, I will ground it in the reality of teachers' voices.

THE LATIN VOICE

Freire: The Foundation

Let me introduce you to the Paulo Freire I love. I have a tiny tape recorder that often can be found on my windowsill above the kitchen sink. When I begin to lack courage, or when I need more patience, I play only one tape:

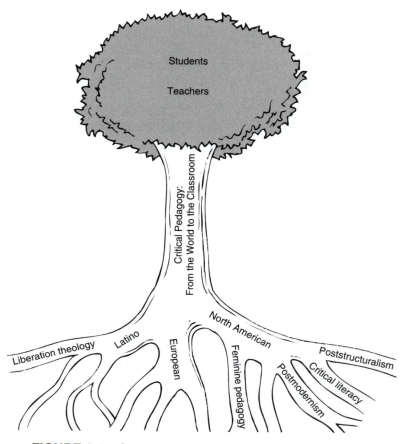

FIGURE 3.1 Critical roots

Paulo Freire (1993). This is a recording I made of him speaking to several thousands of people in southern California — but, when I listen to this tape, I still feel as though he were speaking only to me. During this presentation, he spoke of two concepts: teaching and learning. As I listened, the seeds for this book were planted. As we were walking away, Dawn said, "Mom, he's just like Gandhi, only with clothes on."

For me, he is the quintessential teacher and learner. Freire has taught many things to many people all over the world. When I read his words, when I hear his words, I learn and relearn to focus on teaching and learning that is rigorous and joyful (Freire, 1994; Gadotti, 1994). When I walk into a class or a presentation, I am thinking: rigorous and joyful, rigorous and joyful, rigorous and joyful.

Much of multicultural critical pedagogy in North America today stands on the shoulders of this giant: Paulo Freire. He taught me the difference between "reading the word and the world." During the 1960s, Freire conducted a national literacy campaign in Brazil for which he eventually was jailed and exiled from his own country. He not only taught the peasants to read, he taught them to understand the reasons for their oppressed condition. The sounds, letters, and words from the world of his adult learners were integrated and codified. Ideas, words, and feelings joined together to generate a powerful literacy that was based on the learners' lived experiences. The Brazilian peasants learned to read the words rapidly because they had already read the world, and their world was the foundation for reading the words. Traditionally, literacy has been the process of reading only the word. Emancipatory literacy is reading the world. Freire was not jailed and exiled because he taught peasants to "read the word," but because he taught the subordinate class to critically read the world (Freire & Macedo, 1987). Freire taught the peasants to use their knowledge and their literacy to examine and reexamine the surrounding power structures of the dominant society.

Freire teaches that no education is politically neutral. Traditionally, teachers (that would include me) have assumed that we don't have to bother with politics; teaching is our concern. I see on my resume that one of the first state conference presentations I ever gave was entitled "Teaching, I Love. It's the Politics, I Hate." I now think that I was pretty naive, and maybe even elitist, to think that teaching and learning could possibly take place in a vacuum. Every time we choose curriculum, we are making a political decision. What will I teach, and what won't I teach? The social, cultural, and political implications are great. After reading Freire, a local teacher wrote me this note on E-mail.

Freire left me with a new insight. I had never thought about the role of passivity. Before, I did not look at passivity as being active. This oxymoron is new to me. I am learning that these contradictions are confounding and enlightening.

Schools are social; they are filled with real people who live in real communities and have real concerns. People with multiple perspectives send their kids to schools. Teaching and learning are a part of real life, and real life includes politics and people. Schools do not exist on some elevated pure plain of pedagogy away from the political perspectives of people. If two friends sit down for a social visit, politics is a part of it. If hundreds of kids from a neighborhood come to school, politics is a part of it. Paulo Freire recognized this before many others in education. If educators state that they are neutral, then they are on the side of the dominant culture. "Passivity is also a powerful political act," a student said to me. Teaching is learning.

Traditionally, the *strong* voice of school has been very homogeneous along the lines of race, class, and gender. Historically, the *strong* have been the A Team, and the *weak* have been the B Team. The *weak* have been underrepresented and not heard. This is changing, and change is hard. Twenty-five years ago I wrote in a private journal that I thought we would go "kicking and screaming" into a multicultural society at the turn of the century. I remember feeling rather neutral, distant, and clever when I wrote it. I had no idea how difficult it would be for us as a society to change. Change makes the *strong* feel weakened, and the *weak* feel strengthened.

Demographically, the world has changed. And, nowhere are those changes experienced more profoundly than in classrooms today. Many classes are filled with traditional teachers and nontraditional students, conventional teachers and nonconventional students. The past is past; it is not necessarily bad, but it is past. We all must move forward. We cannot continue to use old answers for new questions. The questions have changed, and together, we are seeking new answers for new questions. Critical pedagogy has helped me rethink old questions, and Paulo Freire has helped me search for new answers.

This year I had an experience in the Minneapolis airport that demonstrated to me how much change has taken place. I had three hours to wait, and I spent the time walking, looking, and trying to enjoy myself. I was very aware of a most uncomfortable feeling; I felt out-of-sync, a vague feeling of apprehension and uneasiness. As I became more and more aware of my feelings, I tried to analyze why I was feeling that way. After a couple of hours of strolling and musing, it hit me like a ton of bricks: Everyone looked just like me; it was like a world full of Joan clones. One generation ago, a homogeneous world was the only world I knew. It made me reflect on how much had actually changed, and how we change with the changes. It's moments like these that give me hope.

Labeling Freire.   Paulo Freire has been labeled "the most labeled educator." He has been labeled Marxist, idealistic, liberal, national-developmentalist, new schoolist, inductivist, spontaneist, nondirectivist, and Catholic neo-anarchist (Gadotti, 1994, p. 126). My spell-check has trouble with some of these labels; I do, too. I have heard him called a communist, a revolutionary, a philosopher, and a genius. Lots of labels. He has been called the authentic intellectual in our world, an ancient sage, and in his own words, humble warrior of the spirit (Gadotti, 1994). Of all the labels for Paulo Freire that I have heard, the one I love the best is the one my spell-check uses: *Freer*. Yes!

Labels I Love to Hate.   Paulo Freire and Tove Skutnabb-Kangas were two of the first voices I read who made me stop and think about our use of labels in North American educational institutions. It was one of those hey-I-never-thought-of-that-experiences for me. For example, think of the word *minority*. From Freire (Freire & Macedo, 1987) I learned that it is often laden with connotations of less — less of something.

Do you see how ideologically impregnated the term "minority" is? When you use "minority" in the U.S. context to refer to the majority of people who are not part of the dominant class, you alter its semantic value. When you refer to "minority" you are, in fact, talking about the "majority" who find themselves outside the sphere of political and economic dominance. In reality, as with many other words, the semantic alteration of the term "minority" serves to hide the many myths that are part of the mechanism sustaining cultural dominance. (pp. 124 – 125)

Recently, a teacher was complaining that her students "weren't intelligent" and "couldn't learn." However, she was particularly annoyed because "most are minorities." Wait. Most are minorities? Then, wouldn't they be majorities? Traditionally, I think we thought of the words *minority* and *majority* in a numerical sense. Minority meant less; majority meant more. Something has changed. If not numbers, then what in the world are we talking about? More and more, my sense is that when schools complain that they have so many "minorities," the hidden message is that the "minorities" have less value than the "majorities."

The legacy of Paulo Freire is pushing me to unlearn other labels. I know of a junior high school that proudly boasts of its "Potentially At-Risk Program." I can almost guarantee that all the kids placed in that program will end up "at risk." Labels can lead to tracks, which are an insidious form of social sorting. Sometimes, we don't like to be bothered with this issue of labels. I think we need to bother ourselves more with the hidden implications of our language. What we say matters. The rationale of that's-the-way-we've-always-said-it just doesn't work for me anymore. However, sometimes the issue of labels and its devastating effects is exceedingly clear for almost everyone to understand. For example, a teacher told me she was visiting another classroom in her school. Within the first half hour of her visit, the teacher of that class had pointed out the "losers" in his room. Every student in the class heard his comments, and she noted that every one of them was either brown, black, or poor.

THE EUROPEAN VOICE

Critical pedagogy also has been influenced by voices from Europe. In the following, I will trace the roots of multicultural critical pedagogy in North American schools back to social and political contexts of other places and other times. The theory of reproduction, which started as an economic, political, and social idea, continues to thrive in schools today, but it is much more difficult to see and to understand than when it was a faraway idea in the history books. This part of the chapter will look at the early ideas of resistance that are alive and well in critical pedagogy of today.

Gramsci

The word *hegemony*, the domination of one group over another, can be traced to the Italian social theorist Gramsci. He felt that hegemony was how societal institutions maintained their power, even by force if necessary. Gramsci (1971) felt it was important for educators to recognize and acknowledge the existing oppressive structures inherent in schools. Power is a fundamental societal issue. As Western industrial societies grow more sophisticated, power is less likely to be used in a physical manner and more likely to be used in subtle ways that are harder to see because even the dominated group is partially supporting the process.

If Gramsci could walk into the following classroom, I wonder if he would say the teacher is unknowingly using her hegemonic powers to hurt children of lower socioeconomic families. I think so.

> *Linda and Jean were visiting each other. Their children attend the same neighborhood school. Suddenly, Linda's five-year-old son runs into the living room to show off his new clothes. He proudly turns around and grins from ear to ear.*
>
> *"You are going to look so handsome when you start school," Jean said to David as he beamed.*
>
> *"I really don't have the money to spend on new clothes, but he is going to be well dressed when he goes to school. His teacher is into beautiful children. She just relates better to children with new clothes than to children in raggedy hand-me-downs," Linda said to Jean.*
>
> *"Where did you ever get such a terrible idea?" Jean asked. "I was a volunteer in her class last year. She would focus on the students who had the nice clothes and ignore the others. I could see that all too well. So David is going to be one of the best-dressed boys in the class," she responded matter-of-factly.*

Linda is a single mom with four children and a limited budget. She recognizes the hidden messages of money in this classroom. Because she sees critically and articulates clearly, she is already beginning her own counter-hegemony.

Other examples of hegemony are twelve- and thirteen-year-old girls who suddenly begin to do poorly in math and science courses. It is not that girls are less intelligent; it is that they are partially supporting the process of believing that boys know more about numbers and problem solving. Another example of hegemony I sometimes hear is Spanish-dominant families saying that they don't want their children in Spanish bilingual classes. From Gramsci, I have learned that in subtle and insidious ways, we can all be a part of maintaining myths.

Marx

The economic and social ideas of Karl Marx form important roots of critical pedagogy. Marx believed education was being used as an insidious vehicle for institutionalizing elite values and for indoctrinating people into unconsciously maintaining these values.

Marxist thought challenges the way in which the dominant ideology is reproduced through the use of *myths* (Macedo, 1994), which offer a sound bite to legitimize processes of oppression. One is the myth of a classless America — we're-all-alike-and-all-have-equal-access-to-opportunity-in-this-great-land. I have noticed that people who believe this tend not to hobnob with the folks who know it isn't true. Myths are used as tools so the have-nots will affirm and support the processes that benefit the haves. A glaring example is the way George Bush in 1988 campaigned on the notion of a classless America while at the same time fought for a capital gains tax to benefit the rich and threatened to veto a tax cut for the middle class (Macedo, 1994). The gulf between the social groups continues to widen, although some would have us think the gulf is not there.

Marx's ideas of reproduction are reflected in every classroom with subtle and hidden processes in which social classes are classified and grouped. Schools call it tracking. Sometimes social classes suddenly are acknowledged even by those who have traditionally denied them. They are publicly identified if they can be used to legitimize processes that hurt other groups of kids. For example, during an in-service teacher education workshop, a group of teachers was discussing what they could do to serve more effectively the needs of bilingual kids. The principal of this school, who had been a very reluctant participant throughout the in-service, could stand it no longer and suddenly announced in a loud voice to the group:

> *"Oh, we don't have any LEPs in our school. The problem we have is poor white trash."*

The teachers passively hung their heads — I think with shame — but, they did not challenge her. My hunch is that the "poor white trash" in this school will be tracked for as long as they can stand to stay in school.

Labeling Marx.   Whereas Freire had many labels, I think it would be safe to label Marx a Marxist. So the question becomes: What is a Marxist? What does it feel like to be in a Marxist classroom? I recently had the opportunity to ask these questions of students in a writing composition class.

What does a Marxist, the teacher, in this classroom look like? A lot like several hundreds of others teachers whom I have known. He was sitting in a circle with 25 students who had lots of books on their desks and appeared (to me) to be eager to learn, which I later found to be true. The teacher explained to me that the class was not studying Marx; rather, they were simply teaching and learning with a Marxist approach. My original question began to change a little: What is a Marxist approach to pedagogy? The students jumped right into the dialogue and told me.

A Marxist Approach to Pedagogy

It reignited my desire to learn.

It forces me to think.

Anyone can ask and answer questions.

We take time to learn.

It is applicable to my life.

It connects me to my imagination.

It always seeks other views.

The students discussed their frustration with other classes in which they had to write down everything the professor said and then return the same knowledge on a test. They spoke of their yearning to know of multiple paths to teaching and learning.

Freire and Marx provide deep roots for critical pedagogy that are reflected in learners turning their beliefs into behaviors for self and social transformation. The ideas we grapple with are not just for the safe confines of the four walls of the classroom. The whole idea is to improve the quality of life for ourselves and for others in our community. The mere momentum of the status quo will keep us in a vacuum unless we walk out the door and seek other ways of knowing.

One young woman explained to us that this was not her first pedagogical experience with a Marxist approach. She said that she had a similar experience in the fourth grade when the students in her class were encouraged to investigate everything and anything. As she spoke, I was thinking: Inquiry. Inquiry. Inquiry. She vividly recalled the teacher who had a secret box that he said held the key to their learning. The box had taken on a rather magical aura as the students were so eager to know the secret of the box, the secret to their own learning. Eventually, they were to learn that the box contained a mirror.

These students in the composition class were actively engaged with new ideas; they were socially generating new knowledge; they were cogitating; and they were reading challenging books. This all seemed good to me. So, I asked them: If this pedagogy is working so well, why is Marx the bad guy to so many North Americans?

"He messes up the control," one young man quietly said. His classmates nodded their heads in agreement.

I have noticed that when the subject of Marx comes up, a confrontation often follows. Confrontation is great sport for some, particularly those who have more control and power. Confrontation is more difficult for others, particularly those who have less control and power. Marx hands us a mirror and makes us look at our traditional patterns of control in schooling, patterns that run along the lines of race, class, and gender.

The Frankfurt School of Critical Theory

The Frankfurt School of Critical Theory of the 1940s believed schools were a vehicle for reproduction (a.k.a., tracked for life) whereby the workers who were needed in the existing power structures of society were prepared. These critical theorists postulated that the schools not only reproduce what society needs, but the corresponding social and personal demeanor as well. Gee (1990) updates this notion and shares his perspective:

> Schools have historically failed with nonelite populations and have thus replicated the social hierarchy, thereby advantaging the elites in the society. This has ensured that large numbers of lower socioeconomic and minority people engage in the lowest level and least satisfying jobs in the society (or no jobs), while being in a position to make few serious political or economic demands on the elites. Indeed, the fact that *they* have low literacy skills can be used (by themselves and the elites) as a rationale for them to be in low-level jobs and the elites in higher level ones . . . . (p. 31)

Sometimes reproduction is easier to see than other times. Tracking is often one of the institutionalized processes that is very visible, but the reproduction of the status quo and the existing power structures are more invisible. In one district I know, they have the usual tracks: *snob* track, *poor-white-trash* track, Spanish/Portuguese track, and a new one that I just recently became aware of, the middle-class track. Remember, I do not make up these stories; these are words I repeatedly hear. The students who are tracked through these *colored* institutionalized processes reflect and reproduce themselves again and again.

TEACHER #1: Yes, it's yellow for the Asians, red for the Mexicans. It's the way they segregate the kids.

TEACHER #2: Yeah. That way if an Asian moves to another school, he'll be on the same track.

TEACHER #3: Yes, that's how they segregate at our school, too. Yellow for the Asians, red for the Mexican, and green for the *white trash*.

Tove Skutnabb-Kangas

Let me introduce you to Tove Skutnabb-Kangas, whom I know and love. She often brings out a strong response when people meet her, and the same was true for me. I had read her works for years, so I was prepared for the power of her thoughts, but I was not prepared for her personality. No one had ever told me.

Since the day I met her, the Easter Bunny and Malcolm X will forever be wedded in my mind. Let me explain. We were in a county school office presentation room; tables, chairs, and teachers filled the room. When I walked in, I noted a general air of excitement and happiness. I recognized the sound I heard: the happy hum of learning. Tove was moving among the teachers as they worked at tables; I could hear thoughtful questions and chuckles of joy throughout the room. I stood in the back of the room for about 10 minutes and simply enjoyed watching and experiencing the entire environment. "So, this is the famous Tove Skutnabb-Kangas," I thought.

Tove is of medium height and build; she has blonde curly hair that does exactly what it wants to do; and, she has round, round cheeks with the pinkest skin I have ever seen. Not white, but pink. The minute I met her, I thought of the round little nose and cheeks of the Easter Bunny. When she smiles, her face lights up the room. On that day, she was wearing brilliant colors with a long flowing skirt that had sequins sewn in so there was a kind of twinkle and reflection as she walked. She had on a fuscia T-shirt, with a multicolored scarf and a darker jacket. For me, there is this aura of a cuddly Easter Bunny about Tove. A very powerful Easter Bunny, indeed.

She came to our campus and worked with teachers and learners in the area. While she was here, she met and visited with one of my male colleagues who had previously heard me describe her. When she left, he said, "Easter Bunny, huh? Maybe a pink Malcolm X." Her ideas are strong, and her love is soft. When I see her, which is never often enough, I am filled with joy. We laugh and hug, and hug and laugh. Then, we begin to discuss powerful ideas.

I have noticed that not everyone reacts to Tove the way I did during my initial encounter with her. In fact, sometimes the power of her ideas gives people a tummy ache. Sharon, a teacher/grad student, shares her story.

> *I first met Tove at a conference in San Francisco. I sat in the front row of the enormous auditorium. I didn't want to miss a word, an inference, a smile.*
>
> *Soon, an official of the conference introduced Tove Skutnabb-Kangas, and I immediately noticed her rosy cheeks. Everyone applauded as Tove stepped up to the microphone and began talking loudly about education and language. Where was this soft cuddly bunny rabbit I had heard about? I was so confused. I sat up in my chair so I could try to grasp the words. What? I, as a teacher, was cutting off the native language of my bilingual students? Me, who is so dedicated? My preconceived notions exploded! Well, yes it is true, I only speak English, and I don't know the language of my students.*
>
> *I sat up even straighter and thought seriously about leaving the room. How could I get out of here? And, my professor was sitting two seats away. This message was not comfortable for me to hear. I mean, how could I be hurting children?*
>
> *I listened painfully and quickly left the room when Tove finished. I was enraged, hurt, confused, and angry. Later that week in class, we talked about the conference. My professor began talking about how wonderful it was to listen to Tove. All of a sudden she said, "Sharon, tell your colleagues about Tove." I could feel my face turning red, and I had to say, "Well, I really didn't care for her. I thought she was very loud and angry."*
>
> *For the next year, I read, reflected, mused, read, reflected, mused before I came to terms with my feelings. Tove was not saying that I was a bad teacher, only the fact that I was not meeting the academic needs of multilingual students in their primary language.*
>
> *Yes, I could teach them in English, I could give them love and build their self-esteem. I could not, however, give them what they really needed to succeed in an English-speaking world: literacy and cognitive development. Even as I worked with the students on the oral English development, they would start to fall behind their classmates cognitively and linguistically.*

Now, you have met two Toves, or at least one very complex person. You will have to draw your own conclusions. Let me share with you a more formal introduction to Tove Skutnabb-Kangas, the internationally known Finnish linguist. She is a critical theorist with deep roots throughout many parts of Europe. She has worked throughout the world as a sociolinguistic and a change-agent. However, because of her numerous trips to the United States, many (like me) have come to know her almost as if she were a part of the North American voice. She has challenged many of us to think and re-think in critically relevant ways. She consistently asks us to look again at the processes by which the norm gets normalized.

In her writings and her presentations, she has raised the issue of linguistic genocide in our schools. Students enter our schools speaking languages from all over the world; 12 years later, they leave our school, speaking only English. Then, we immediately want them to go to college and study *foreign* languages. Tove asks us to rethink this practice. And, she asks us to consider why it is taking place. Other countries often use direct and brutal tactics to prevent minority languages. In the United States our methods are indirect and more effective. When students are not served in the mother tongue, and when students are not allowed to use their own language to construct meaning, we are all part of the process that normalizes the majority use of English and disenfranchises all other languages. Or, as Tove has repeatedly said: "We kill languages every day in our classes."

I cannot imagine what it must be like for a five-year-old to go to school and learn that this language of family love, of Mom, Dad, Grandma, and Grandpa, is bad. What must it feel like to be a small child and feel shame for your own mother's language? Five-year-olds read the world well and understand quickly that their family's language is bad. This is why they learn to say: "I don't speak Spanish." Shame does terrible things; anger follows shame? (This unlearning is not always comfortable.) I think when Tove raises this question with schools in the United States, she is moving us institutionally to problem posing. Traditionally, the dominant culture does not respond well to this type of probing, thoughtful activity.

Declaration: Kids Need to Learn.   Tove continues to campaign for the United Nations to adopt the Declaration of Children's Linguistic Human Rights. Before I share it, let me explain something about Tove to you. English is not her first, nor second, nor third language. Every time I ask her how many languages she speaks, reads, writes, and understands, we never get to the end of the answer. She always starts telling me stories about the languages along the way. But, I have noticed that she needs more than her own 10 fingers to do the counting. Even though English is not her first language, she is highly sensitive to gender-specific language that had, until recently, been so entrenched in the English language. In her writing, she has long used only the feminine pronoun as a little prod to help us move to a more equitable approach to gender-free language. I have some men friends who are very sensitive to this and really offended. Feels good to me.

Tove, like many of us, believes that kids need to learn. She noted early in her writing that we don't learn what we don't understand. Therefore, she is an international leader in persuading the United Nations to adopt the following declaration.

Declaration of Children's Linguistic Human Rights

1. Every child should have the right to identify with her original mother tongue and have her identification accepted and respected by others.
2. Every child should have the right to learn the mother tongue fully.
3. Every child should have the right to choose when she wants to use the mother tongue in all official situations.

One of the best experiences I ever had with this declaration happened with the departmental secretary/assistant. Sheri and I see and know in very different ways, but we laugh and have a great time learning together. Two years ago I remember when I first hung a laminated copy of this declaration on the wall above my desk. On more than one occasion, I was aware that Sheri was musing on it, but not mentioning it. This week, as I was walking out the door, Sheri looked at it and quietly said, "Makes sense to me, Joan." I smiled and thought a lot about patience on my way home.

A Team and B Team. Another idea of Tove's, which has affected critical pedagogy in North America, is her concept of the A Team and B Team. Tove speaks to the issues of power with her construct of the A Team and the B Team. The A Team, which controls the power and material resources, continually invalidates and marginalizes the voice of the B Team. This is the way the A Team socially constructs knowledge and maintains its own power.

Pada is a young Hmong-American woman. She has successfully finished her undergraduate studies, she has her teaching credential, and she is now a graduate student. She told me a story about discovering the A and B teams when she arrived in the United States.

When I started high school in the United States, my achievement was high and my command of the English language fairly good. However, I was still terrified of all the tests the schools gave upon entering school. The first battery of tests was to determine which track was best for me: ESL track, B track, or A track. I was placed on the B track, which was designed to prepare students for a vocational career. I felt like the teachers thought I was incompetent. They gave us very little homework, and hardly any real reading and real writing. I remember having to memorize lists of words and their definitions. I could see that the students in A track were always doing more interesting work; I could see that the A track was used to prepare people for college, which was my dream. Every time I tried to get into the A track, my counselor would remind me about my initial entry scores on the exams. I was achieving on B track, but that didn't seem to matter to anyone.

During my second year of high school, my counselor finally allowed me to try A track. However, he continually discouraged me and made me bring letters of support from teachers in order to make the transfer. At that time in my life, I did not understand the meaning of words such as socialization practices, schooling, and teacher expectations, but I could understand that I was being programmed for less than my dream.

A few years ago when I first came into contact with the idea of the A Team and the B Team, I decided to consciously create an A Team and a B Team on the first night of one of my classes. The experience was so powerful that it took us a few weeks to recover. The class of 38 arrived at 5 P.M. We were in a large room with all of the chairs screwed to the floor in straight rows. The teachers/grad students drifted in and greeted each other. Those who knew me and had been in my classes before began by hugging friends, visiting, renewing friendships, and mostly moving towards the chairs in the front to the room. Before everyone was seated, I announced that those who had been in my classes before should sit in the front chairs, and those who had not should sit towards the back. Everyone immediately complied. The front of the room continued with happy noise; the back of the room became quieter. We started class, and I consciously directed my comments to those in the front of the room; those in the back received only token attention. For the next two hours, we continued like this: I would initiate an idea or a thought and ask the students to discuss it. After their discussion, I would ask for whole-group sharing, but I mostly called on only those in the front. I consciously tried to assign status, power, and prestige to those in the front. I behaved as if they knew more and as if their knowledge was more valuable. They thrived. The back of the room became quieter and quieter. Soon I was able to see angry, frustrated looks. During the small-group activities, I could tell they were sharing their anger with each other; I ignored it and walked among the students in the front of the room, who couldn't understand why I was making the new students feel so bad.

After the two hours, I couldn't take it any longer. The front of the room was confused; the back of the room angry. I asked how many of them were teachers; there were 38 teachers in the room. I asked them how many of them were involved with tracking in their class; 38 were involved with tracking. I asked why. The front and back explained to me that they had to do it because some students were *ahead of* and *knew more* than other students. They still did not see the connection to our class. I asked the names of the various tracks: yellow, red, green, blue. They all knew which students went in which track. I asked them if their assumptions about students made a difference in their students' achievement. The front and the back agreed: Our tracks reflect what the students knew.

Although I could tell by looking at their faces, I asked the back of the room how they were feeling: furious, angry, worthless, and finally, ready to drop the class. The front of the room still could not understand why I was making the new students feel so badly. Finally, I just told them that I had created an A Team and a B Team so they could experience it. *Experiencing* is different from *knowing about*. The students in this class are all teachers who *know about* tracking, but when they *experienced* it, they did not like it.

Tracking is so institutionalized in the geographical area where I live that the very thought of challenging it is almost considered heresy.[1] Even the B Team in my class wanted to legitimize it and rationalize it. It took three more classes of dialogue and reading and writing before I felt that the class had come together as a whole, and they could see that I had manipulated them and the context into the haves and the have-nots. I had consciously reproduced a reflection of their world and their individual classrooms. I had socially sorted on purpose to make a point that A Teams and B Teams always work to the advantage of the A Team. Five-year-olds know the difference between the buzzards and the blessed. It doesn't matter what color you label the track.

Lucille, an African American grad student, always knew her elementary teachers thought she was on the B Team. But when she was in junior college, she was amused to find she had been placed on yet another B Team. Only this time, it had a new name, the Lazy Tongues. She was placed in an ESL phonics class with Spanish, Chinese, and Japanese speakers; the professor referred to them as LEPs; Lucille and the other African Americans were the Lazy Tongues. Lucille now believes that this is the way her institution reproduced the existing superstructure, or the A Team and the B team.

What in the world does reproduction of the existing superstructure have to do with classroom teachers? Critical pedagogs often speak and write about schools maintaining and recreating social status and power. For example, if one group of students is labeled *gifted* and another group *limited*, which group benefits? I know a school that divides the *limiteds* into *low limiteds* and *high limiteds*. Apparently, the *high limiteds* would be the "A Team *of* the B Team" in this case. I think that we teachers often don't realize the role we play in this. We have a tendency to think that others do it, but not us. However, if we are creating (consciously or unconsciously) A Teams and B Teams in our classes, we are also a part of reproducing the existing social, cultural, and political power bases.

How does this history of critical pedagogy relate to the everyday life of a classroom teacher? Look around your own school and ask yourself these questions?

1. Who is on the A Team and who is on the B Team? What part might I be playing in the reproduction and maintenance of the two teams?
2. Which students are meaningfully and purposefully interacting to generate more knowledge?
3. Who is doing fill-in-the-blank dittos? Why?
4. Am I unconsciously taking part in the selection and maintenance of the A Team at my school because of my silence?
5. Do we track? Why? Which track is best? Why?

Critical pedagogy relates fundamentally to every teacher and to every student every day. These are basic questions and issues that we live everyday. However, many times we have been so schooled, so institutionalized to believe that we are helpless to make a difference in our own environment. If not us, who? Schools R us. Critical pedagogy enables us to stop the *yeah-buts* and to begin to recognize our own power as professionals. Critical pedagogy gives us the power to understand that we must do the very best where we are today. We cannot fix every educational problem in the world, but we can live our own beliefs in our own communities. Critical pedagogy is the power that leads us from silence to voice.

I will conclude my introduction to Tove Skutnabb-Kangas with one last story. She and I keep a running list of who can find the most damaging, dreadful, despicable label. I have a new one that she has not seen, but will when she reads this. I recently read a document that left our university and went to a state agency. In the document I found a new label under the category of diversity: It was *differing gender*. I guess that would be Tove and me, and it would place us on the B Team. Top that one, Tove!

VYGOTSKY

Who is this Russian psychologist who keeps reemerging in my life and tugging me to my next developmental level? Each time I remeet him, I relearn one of his most fundamental lessons: That which I can do with someone else today, I can do alone tomorrow. A small technicality before we continue: Most of Russia is not in Europe, but for my purposes here, a close neighbor is good enough. Earlier I demonstrated how I had to use his legacy of thought and language before I was able to begin to internalize the language and thoughts of critical pedagogy. Figure 3.2 visualizes this process. Now I would like to tell you more about his ideas.

Why Vygotsky?

Vygotsky is just the person to tug us beyond tradition. He is just the person to lead us back to the future. The past is not bad; much can be learned from it (as in this particular case), but the past is just that: past. And, as teachers, we have to teach tomorrow, not yesterday. Just as he did with his contemporaries, he can help us rethink our past practices; he can lead us to rethink our past, our present, and our future to ensure that our practices reflect today and tomorrow.

The broader the perspective we bring to ideas, the better the idea. Ideas are improved when people of highly diverse groups gather together and share their perspectives. The broader the representation, the better the democracy. We are called by the legacy of Vygotsky to surround and improve our ideas with a broad spectrum of thought.

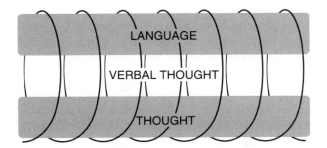

FIGURE 3.2 Visualization of the relationship between language and thought, based on Vygotsky

As we experience global demographic shifts, a new social context compels us to regenerate theory and practice, thus creating our own personal praxis that informs and empowers teaching and learning in a diverse society. This search for philosophy and practice, which draws upon the strengths of many cultures in society while promoting cognitive development, leads us to Lev Vygotsky.

I find this story from the past has the potential to lead us to our future as educators. From his life, I learn and relearn valuable lessons that relate to students and classrooms. I discover and rediscover courage in the midst of challenging sociocultural, political, and historical changes.

Who Is This Educator from the Past Who Tugs Us into Our Future?

My historical perspective of Vygotsky has been influenced by many years and many classes of reading about Vygotsky. When I think of him, the faces of former professors pop into my mind. I remember many of the stories, people, and places that have enriched my understandings of Vygotskian thought. However, for the following historical snapshot, I am primarily indebted to Guillermo Blanck (Moll, 1990) and Alex Kozulin (Vygotsky, 1986). Their research is based on the most primary and authoritative sources that are available.

Vygotsky was born in 1896. He suffered greatly and died early. He spent his youth in northern Russia with his middle class Jewish family. During prerevolutionary years in Russia, Jewish families suffered from discrimination. In spite of this repressive environment, he generated a huge pedagogical legacy, which speaks to critical pedagogy of today. As a Jewish teenager in a dominant society that placed a lesser value on being Jewish, discrimination was a part of his life. He drew strength from his culturally grounded values and identity.

From these early years of his life, we are reminded of the importance of family involvement in all aspects of education. Families are the first and most important teachers in any child's life. Education does not take place only in our classrooms; we must open the doors to include the voices of all families. In addition to his learning within his own family, Vygotsky's education was enhanced by the Socratic method of question and answer. His genius surfaced early in his life. What would happen to this caliber of student in public schools today? Would this type of intellectual ability be recognized and validated?

My reading of his life has given me an appreciation of his courage to follow his nontraditional and unconventional interests. During his college years, the Russian Revolution (1917) was forcing massive societal changes, similar to what we are experiencing in our world today. In 1919 Vygotsky contracted tuberculosis. During these years, the Russian people suffered from famine, hunger, and cold. Surprisingly, great intellectual growth was flourishing in the midst of these hardships.

From the social-historical context of his life, which included collaboration, dialogue, and hardship, he began to reinterpret ideas from the standpoint of his own lived experience. During this final phase of his life, his condition deteriorated, yet he continued to be a prolific writer and scholar. In 1934, at the age of 37, he died from tuberculosis.

Vygotsky's life story is a source of inspiration for me. I hope the same is true for you. By looking at the historical context of his life, we are better able to understand his educational ideas, which constantly emphasize the fundamental importance of context and culture on language and learning. I believe his ideas are equally important for North American schools as we enter the twenty-first century.

The sociocultural context of his life was central to who he was and how he made meaning in his life. As he used language with his family and his friends, his cognition grew. The same is true for each of us. The same is true for every student in our classes. If students are denied the opportunity to use their language, they are denied the opportunity to develop their own cognition. Silence them, and they cannot learn. All students need to talk and listen to one another in academic discussion. Playground language alone will not lead to higher levels of literacy and cognition.

We, as teachers, do not have control over the environment of each one of the students, but we do have the power to create the best sociocultural context within our own classrooms. Six hours a day in an environment that encourages students to use their language in order to create more knowledge can be the difference between success and failure. Students have taught me again and again that even one hour a day can be enough. I doubt that there is a teacher among us who didn't go into education "to make a difference."

If you have not read every word of my history of Lev Vygotsky, it is okay. For you, I have provided a little historical glance. One of the most important things I ever had to relearn and unlearn was that it is okay not to read every word and page of every book, and it is okay not to finish every book.

When thinking about Vygotsky, just remember this: He was born a long time ago; he lived a very short life; he suffered a lot; and he left us a treasured gift with his ideas of teaching and learning.

A View of Vygotsky

1896	Born to a large Jewish family in Russia; grew up in a family of books, and ideas, and conversation; learned by Socratic dialogue.
1913	Entered the university despite restrictive policies against Jewish students.
1917	Russian Revolution; graduated simultaneously from two universities; taught for seven years; intense cultural and intellectual creation; postrevolutionary period of famine; no heat, hunger, reading/writing/talking with Hegel, Marx, Bacon, Descartes, Engels.
1919	Contracted tuberculosis.
1921	Married; had two daughters; intense productivity; magnetic energy.
1925	Finished dissertation; too sick to defend it.
1929–1930	Completed 50 articles.
1934	Died at age 37; Stalin's persecution of intellectuals begins; his writings are banned for 20 years; 180 total works written.
1956	Krushchev lifts ban; his work reemerges and translations begin.
1979	His wife died.
1985	Youngest daughter died; older daughter is still an educational psychologist and is retired and living in Moscow.

Vygotsky's legacy for critical education of today and tomorrow includes three main concepts: (1) sociocultural learning, or the context matters; (2) the zone of proximal development, or our interaction with friends in this context matters; and (3) the relationship between thought and language, or words and ideas used in this context matters.

Sociocultural Learning

In a conversation about real estate, you may have heard about the importance of location, location, location. In teaching and learning, it is context, context, context. The next time you muse on the importance of context in your own teaching and learning, you can thank Vygotsky. For example, how does critical pedagogy play out in Trenton, Topeka, or Turlock? Depends on context. Those who live within a community, those who have experienced a unique (social, historical, cultural, political) context, have understandings that others do not have. Students, teachers, and community members know their questions in distinctive ways; they generate their answers based on their own context. Their questions and answers can be informed from voices in other (social, cultural, historical, political) places, but ultimately context sways conclusions. Anyone who has ever raised teenagers understands the major role that the environment plays in determining one's path.

We hear a lot about sociocultural learning lately, and it tends to have different names that all mean about the same thing: socially grounded learning, social learning, sociocultural-political-historical learning, etc. The basic point is that we generate knowledge in a social context. Learning is social, and sometimes noisy. When we don't understand something, we visit with a friend and begin to understand better. What happens when you are sitting in a presentation, and you have been talked at, talked at, and talked at? You love it when the speaker finally finishes so you can visit with your friends about your ideas. I hope reading this book will make you want to talk about it in your own context. Learning is social.

The primacy of being human is how we use language in social contexts to make meaning. As we talk, we manipulate and mediate our language and our thoughts, which leads us to higher cognitive processes. As we talk, we get smarter — with a few notable exceptions that pop into my mind. All of the meaning that we generate and mediate is socially and culturally grounded. Teachers who understand this are guiding students, rather than transmitting knowledge. Students are actively generating knowledge rather than passively storing information for possible future use.

None of this takes place in isolation. As each of us experiences life, we are influenced by, and we influence the surrounding environment. Just as Vygotsky's life was surrounded by many variables that influenced him and his ideas, we also are surrounded by a larger world that touches each of us.

In the following picture of social learning, I will use *sociocultural* to portray the Vygotskian perspective. This picture of sociocultural learning will focus on Pablo, a sixth-grade migrant student from Mexico who is in school in the United States. The purpose of the following story is to view the classroom as an entity influenced by the larger world that surrounds each of our students.

Pablo. In the back of the sixth-grade classroom, Pablo sat alone. His jacket covered his head to shut out the classroom and the world during the first two weeks of class. He did not speak to his new classmates, nor did they speak to him. Any attempt by the teacher to draw him into interaction with others was met with resistance on his part, as well as on the part of the other students. The context of his life had influenced him, and likewise he influenced those around him. Much of the world had treated Pablo badly. Because he had been shifted from town to town, he did not want to make ties with anyone for fear that these ties would soon be broken by yet another move to a different school. Instead, he sat at his desk, using his jacket as a shield to isolate him from anyone who dared to get too close. Pablo is surrounded by many factors, as seen in Figure 3.3, that touch his life. He is in the middle of a larger sociocultural context. The world has sent him many messages; he has read his world.

Some, in education, would blame Pablo for not doing his homework, for not sitting up straight, for not *caring* about learning. However, we cannot view Pablo in isolation; we have to look at all the influences that affect Pablo on a daily basis. This particular student cares a lot; it is just that no one in this school has learned it yet.

After many years of being moved from one teacher to another, in and out of resource and special education classes, Pablo found a home in a sixth-grade mainstream classroom. He was able to write only two- or three-word sentences when assisted by his teacher, Kathleen. In her classroom, students working collaboratively took on specific roles to complete the projects. These roles were frequently changed so that all students could realize equal status and opportunity to lead their groups. High emphasis was placed on collaborating and valuing whatever abilities each student brought to the group, as well as arriving at consensus for group reports while maintaining individual accountability. Kathleen was aware that another student in the class, Angela, understood Pablo's language, his culture, and his world. Kath-

FIGURE 3.3   The world of Pablo

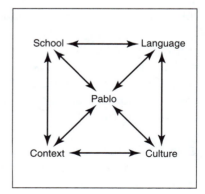

leen placed Pablo in a group of four students: Pablo, Angela, and two of the nicest English-dominant boys in her class. She was hoping that this combination of student resources would be the best possible social situation she could offer this troubled student.

At first, Pablo contributed very little, but taking the coat off his head and joining the group was a victory. Angela offered assistance to him during group activities, and she listened when he spoke.

The two other boys in the group were supportive and yet respectful of his space, and somehow understood that Pablo needed time. Soon, the four began to have fun in their group; they were creating their own group dynamic. After several weeks, Pablo started to take responsibility for himself and his group. Angela translated when necessary, but the group was more and more often focused on the problem-solving activities, and they made meaning in their own way.

Pablo finally removed his coat during class. He next volunteered to be the reporter so he could relate the group findings aloud in front of the class. Initially, he reported with some prompting from Angela. Later, he was able to complete an individual report of their project alone, rather than having to ask for Angela's assistance. After his interactive work in the safe environment of his group, Pablo was able to construct his own paragraph of five sentences based upon what he had learned during the activity. Group learning does not always work for all students, but sometimes it can be very helpful, as in this case.

Pablo eventually worked at levels others had not thought possible. The sociocultural context of the class had a powerful effect on Pablo and his learning. Not only did Pablo construct his knowledge in this classroom, but he was able to begin to reconstruct his world.

When I last saw Pablo, he had moved on to seventh grade at the junior high school. I was driving by his school in the afternoon while students were outside waiting for school buses to take them home. There stood Pablo, alone, in the blistering valley heat, with his coat tightly zipped up, as if to close off the world. Once again the sociocultural context of Pablo had placed in him a vulnerable position. He tightly pulled his coat around his shoulders to protect himself from influences of his new educational world. Sadly, I watched Pablo and was reminded that if we are to reach our potential as a society, each Pablo must have an opportunity to realize maximum potential. Teachers often ask: "What can I do?" Pablo and Vygotsky provide part of the answer. The interrelationship of all students and all languages, in a safe and secure environment, is fundamentally important for literacy and cognitive development It is also important for our future. (Wink, Putney, & Bravo-Lawrence, January/February, 1995).

Zone of Proximal Development (ZPD)

What in the world is the ZPD? Once again, we can turn to Vygotsky and Pablo to discover the answer. Vygotsky said:

> The ZPD is the distance between the actual developmental level as determined by independent problem solving and the level of potential development as determined through problem solving under adult guidance or in collaboration with more capable peers. (Vygotsky, 1978, p. 86)

Pablo's Story: The ZPD in Action

> First, no one thought he could learn.
> Second, he learned with his group.
> Third, he was able to learn alone.

Vygotsky viewed this experience as a key factor affecting the relationship between thought and speech. Students use language to communicate thoughts, and through the social act of verbalizing those thoughts (talking to each other) combine their experiences with those of others. These zones we create in our classes, in our departments, in our communities, and in our homes make a difference in individual lives and in society. They have the potential to lead to self and social transformation.

Thought and Language

The third legacy of Vygotsky relates to the powerful interrelationship between thought and language. The eighth graders in the following class demonstrate the ways in which students use their language to generate thoughts, and how the thoughts affect their language. Words and ideas: it's a two-way street.

Richard.   Richard's social studies class was studying the Preamble to the Constitution. In this classroom of 28 students, 15 are English-dominant, 6 are Spanish-dominant, 4 are Cambodian-dominant, and 3 are Lao-dominant. The text and the language of the classroom is English. Richard and his students have just orally read the Preamble in English. After heterogeneously grouping the students, Richard explained:

> *"Rewrite the Preamble using your own language. Look at the Preamble, pick it apart and put the* thoughts *back together with any* language *that you want to use. Words like everyday talk at home, or outside of school, Spanish, English, Cambodian, Lao. Use street language if you want. Use any language, but just demonstrate the thoughts of the Preamble. Afterwards, in your groups, redo it in English so that I can understand."*
>
> *"Our language? Any language? Just write the ideas?" the students asked.*
>
> *They buzzed with each other about the prospect of writing their thoughts in their languages and then translating them to English.*
>
> *Richard answered, "Write it, agree on it as a group, read it, and explain it. Brainstorm. Put your homo sapien cabezas together. How would you put this in everyday language so you can go to the local market and talk about the Constitution?" After a pause he prompted, "We the people, me and my friends."*
>
> *"Me and my posse?" asked one.*
>
> *"Yes!"*
>
> *"Yo y mis amigos?"*
>
> *"Si."*
>
> *"My buds and I?"*
>
> *"Sure."*

The purpose of this lesson is for the students to relate the language of the Preamble with the embedded thoughts. Marginalized students are often denied the opportunity of full participation in discussing abstract concepts in content areas. In the previous example, Richard organized his classroom and implemented his own pedagogy so all students internalized the abstract concepts of this social studies class. Richard was building on the resources that each student brings to the classroom.

As the students write and talk in their own language they internalize the democratic ideas of the Constitution. This process is multidimensional, boundless, dynamic, and noisy. Language informs thought, and thoughts come to life in language.

For example, in Richard's class, as the students talk and write, the pedagogy shifts from teacher-directed to student-centered. As Richard's pedagogy has demonstrated, he understands that student-generated ideas have the potential to build upon one another and to develop even more thoughts and more language. As we talk, we manipulate, not only our language, but also our thoughts, which leads us to higher cognitive processes. The use of language as an expression of thought is central to developing knowledge and literacy: the heart and soul of critical pedagogy.

In a pluralistic society, the issue of language acquisition is fundamental for all teachers. If students don't get to read and talk in a language they know, they don't get to learn: using our own language makes us smarter — that is why everyone in the world loves their own language. And, when we are smarter, we learn other languages faster. Language develops cognition; words turn into thoughts, and thoughts turn into more words. All students need to talk and listen to each other in social, academic, and problem-solving contexts. Vygotsky's concept of the relationship between thought and language is how I developed my own cognition about critical pedagogy.[2]

Vygotsky's Legacy to Critical Pedagogy

Meaningful dialogue matters.
Our lived experiences make a difference.
Our business is to keep tugging students
to their next cognitive level.
The combination of words and ideas generates
more.

THE NORTH AMERICAN VOICE

When the Latin and European critical perspective arrived in the United States, it was nourished by two schools of thought that had a long history in North American educational theory: reconstructionism and progressivism. A critical educational approach had a waiting audience of those who believed that the purpose of education was to continually reconstruct society. Critical theory and Freirian thought joined with democratic ideals, which were central to progressivism. Social reform was inherent in the improvement of schools. The Latino and European critical perspective shared with the progressivists a belief that all of education is value-laden and morally grounded. Dewey's progressive ideas were fertile ground for the seed of critical theory from Europe and Latin America.

Dewey

Dewey said it best: "Accept the child where the child is." Critical pedagogy of today in North America is grounded in this legacy from Dewey. If we could all remember this simple educational principle, how much better our system would be. But sometimes we forget. The following is a description of a family night at the beginning of the school year for the first graders. During the evening, one of the parents asked the teacher:

PARENT: Where do you begin? Do you begin with what the students know?

TEACHER: Oh no, we start on chapter 4; the first three chapters are just review, and I don't want to waste my time with that. If the students aren't there yet, they don't belong in my class.

Run, families, run! And, I know that this teacher studied Dewey in her credential program. She forgot. We continue to forget another lesson from Dewey: "Accept the child as the child is."

K TEACHER: I just don't know what else to do. Esmeralda just sits there. She never says anything. She never takes part in any "regular" activities. She would rather sit alone in her seat all day, I guess.

TEACHER #2: Well, she would do better if she could speak English.

K TEACHER: All the students would do better if they came to school speaking English. In any case, our jobs would be easier.

TEACHER #2: Still you would think that Esmeralda's parents would teach her English. But, I guess that's supposed to be our problem, too.

Accepting who the students are is sometimes very difficult for teachers. Sometimes teachers don't want the students of today; they want the students of yesterday. It's not going to happen. I think that Dewey meant for us to accept the whole child whatever race, class, gender, language, culture. When teachers can't accept who the child is, they sometimes want to blame it on others — like the child or parents. I think this tells us more about the teacher than the child and the parents.

Every educator has studied the effects of progressivism and reproduction on the educational system. These are not abstract, historical ideas that can be relegated to a history book, placed on a shelf, and forgotten. These ideas are alive and well today in a new form with a broader historical, cultural, and political base.

Oftentimes, simultaneous and conflicting ideologies move through history together. Yet, another contradiction as we experience change. Today, we would call this polarization; however it is not a new phenomenon. During the days of progressivism and reconstructionism, very divergent ideas existed at the same time. Critical pedagogy often refers to oppositional views as the *other*, which is reflected in the way that schools were historically used to control and to maintain the existing power structure. This is not a new concept on the North American continent. As early as the 1850s, schools were considered to be the most effective method of Americanizing the many immigrants who were coming to the New World for freedom and democracy. Many believed it was the responsibility of the schools, with their European American philosophies, to test the loyalty of "new immigrants," who were the groups that tended to come from southern and eastern Europe and Asia. I immediately can think of several new immigrants I know whose loyalty is being tested today. Can you? Cubberley of Stanford was an eloquent leader of this movement. He felt that to Americanize was to Anglicize. It was the duty of the schools to assimilate the new immigrants as part of the American race (Cremin, 1964). American race? What in the world is that? "Americanism is not, and never was, a matter of race or ancestry" (Roosevelt, as cited in Carnes, 1995).

The social relations of power that take place in schools every day mirror the power relationships of society. It seems we, in schools, are trying to do the same thing. Bowles and Gintis (1976) wrote that there is a simple correspondence between schooling, class, family, and social inequities. Schools are mirrors of society.

The idea of schools reproducing inequalities of society is a part of the critical theory legacy to North American school of today. It is not always an easy, nor welcome, topic for discussion; sometimes it causes great resistance. However, I would only ask that we follow the advice of Goodlad (in Goldberg, 1995), who was reflecting on the words of John Dewey who said: "What the researcher in education must do is to get immersed in the complex phenomena, then withdraw and think about the issues" (p. 85).

Ada

Alma Flor Ada has influenced multiple classrooms and families with her critical approach to teaching and learning. Her influences are particularly felt on the West Coast.

I know we aren't supposed to say this (to use "empower" with an object seems ungrammatical), but Alma Flor Ada *empowers* me. After I am with her, I am braver, smarter, and nicer. She lives her beliefs daily and somehow makes it okay to be whoever you happen to be. In addition, I never go in front of a group to teach unless I have her methodology (Ada, 1988a, 1988b) safely tucked away in the corner of my brain. She calls it the Creative Reading Method, which is far too narrow a description for me. I have found it to be effective in any teaching/learning context.

Instead of the five-step lesson plan, try her approach:

- Descriptive Phase: information is shared by teacher, text, media, etc.
- Personal Interpretation Phase: students grapple with new information based on their lived experiences.
- Critical Phase: invites reflection and critical analysis.
- Creative Phase: theory to practice, connects learning from class to the real world of the student.

In chapter 4, I will provide examples of teachers and learners who are using this methodology in their classrooms. Alma Flor Ada's Creative Reading Method (a.k.a., Alma Flor's emancipatory teaching/learning model) is an approach that every teacher can begin tomorrow. As we enter into transformative pedagogy, it is often difficult to know exactly where to start. Alma Flor's process of the descriptive, personal interpretive, critical, and creative phases provides classroom teachers with a framework in which to discover their own praxis.

McCaleb

How many times have we heard educators say: "*I schedule parent conferences, but the parents won't come. How do we 'do' parental involvement?*" Sudia Paloma McCaleb (1994) is helping educators build community and build books. She asks educators to look within and examine their own assumptions about families and literacies. Recently, a secondary teacher read this book and said to me:

> *I used to think that* these *families were illiterate and didn't care. Now, I know that my assumptions contributed to keeping the families from coming to visit with me.*

For McCaleb, transformative educators are those who view the role of a teacher not as the all-knowing instructor, but rather as a coparticipant in the learning process with students. A Spanish-English bilingual secondary teacher told me:

I held parent conferences last year, and not a single parent came. I thought I had been accessible to parents. However, McCaleb made me realize that the families were actually isolated by the appointment system, yet another hidden gatekeeping process. There I sat in my room alone while Spanish-speaking families were to make appointments in the front office with a secretary who spoke only English.

This year I contacted all the parents and invited them to our first family night. I promised them I would get all notices to them in Spanish, and I gave them the name and phone number of a Spanish-speaking secretary. During the next conference schedule, more than 50 percent of the families came to visit during class, and three parents called later. My goal is get all the parents to come.

Giroux

I have written of the importance of courage and patience in our study of critical pedagogy. You will need both when you begin to read Peter McLaren and Henry Giroux. I was reminded of a raging river on a stormy day when I first read these two critical theorists. Behind those big words you will indeed find big ideas.

The first time I ever read the words of Henry Giroux, I actually thought the book was vibrating. I had never read that type of language, but I must have been ready for those powerful ideas. I could not put the book down. Even as I remember it today, it is like an almost physical and metaphysical experience. I finally got it! We, as teachers, are not to be passive, robotic technocrats who can't do anything because of the administration, or the texts, or the parents, or the students, or the tests. We are to be intellectuals and professionals who take control of our own teaching and learning. Perhaps we can't control society's perception of teachers as *less*, but we can control how we perceive ourselves. My suspicion is that as we begin to come to know ourselves as intellectuals and professionals, and turn those beliefs into behaviors, society will begin to change its perception of us.

Giroux's idea of correspondence, which states that schooling functions to reproduce the class structure of the workplace, reaches back to the thinking of the Frankfurt School's theory of reproduction and to the economic production ideas of Marx. Giroux suggests that even though our roots are in the theory of reproduction and resistance, it is time to move to the *possible* that lies within each of us. He focuses his critical lens on curriculum, which is generated by the students and teachers, and reflects their real world. Building from the Freirian concept, Giroux (1988) states that curriculum is never just a neutral body, a warehouse of knowledge. Rather, curriculum is a way of organizing knowledge, values, relationships of social power. Every time I hear a teacher say, "Yeahbut, the curriculum we have to use is so bad," I hear the words of Giroux in my head. He challenges us to challenge ourselves. We are not passive technocrats devoid of power over curriculum. If the curriculum needs to be challenged, challenge it. If not us, who?

McLaren

Peter McLaren challenges teachers to be courageous moral leaders who understand how knowledge, language, experience, and power are central to society and our classrooms. He asks us to look again with new eyes and see how literacies are used to support the A Team. His theory crystallizes the concept that what we do as teachers is morally and ethically grounded. Students lives are at stake daily in our practice. It matters what we do, and we can do a lot. McLaren's words are an echo of Dewey, who stressed the acceptance of the children on their own terms. Many have written of the teachable moment, but only Peter has described the teachable heart.

In the works of McLaren and Giroux, we continually find an underlying current of the potential in each of us. If you are courageous and patient enough in your reading of their ideas, you will find the hidden "Yes-we-can" message they are sending us. It is this idea that transforms teachers to take action and causes the shift to social and self transformation. They open the door to Freire's conscientization. How ironic that Giroux and McLaren, who are often viewed as theorists, can be the trigger to help us turn our own theory into action.

A Teachable Heart.   When I first heard McLaren (1994) mention this idea, I thought, "Yes, that is the by-product of good teaching and learning." I would like to say that he taught this to me, but really what he did is just affirm what I had previously learned from José of the Tucson phone book fame.

You will remember that José was one of that group of students who taught and learned with me for six consecutive years in Benson? The first year I met José he was in seventh grade and didn't say a word all year; José was very much like an ethnographer in that he participated in and observed everything. José was, and is, a quiet, private, and reserved person. In the eighth grade, José started to talk. In the ninth grade, he spoke and students in the class began to listen. In tenth grade, students in other parts of the high school started to listen. In eleventh grade, the students in student government started to listen. In twelfth grade, the entire community started to listen when he graduated with honors in two languages.

In the spring of his senior year, the students chose to take a national honors test in Spanish and in English so those with high achievement could be given college credit for their knowledge. The test was very demanding and did not look like any of the other tests that José had taken from me during the previous six years. I wanted the test also to reflect some of our shared experiences together.

One of our most memorable teaching/learning experiences had taken place when he was a freshman in high school. One of his classmates had innocently asked: how to say "I love you" in Spanish? in French? in German? in Swahili? The list went on and on. This was a turning point for all of us because we stopped whatever we were *covering* and began to research answers for the questions. For the next several weeks, the students went to libraries, interviewed travelers, and visited with families who had come from other countries. The students could not collect enough information to satisfy them; I was almost running to catch up as I tried to understand what was happening. Of course, we learned more about languages, and cultures, and geography than anything else could have taught us. The students also established a list of 25 different ways to say "I love you." They relished practicing in and out of class. Since that time, I have never been afraid to follow the natural curiosity of students.

Although this activity had not been mentioned in class since their freshman year, when José and his classmates sat down to take the national test, I wanted to include some part of it as a reminder of our very special time together. On the final page of the very long test, I had written in bold letters down the middle of the page:

Translate into as many languages as you can:

I love you. _____

I love you. _____

I love you. _____

I love you. _____

I love you. _____

I love you. _____

I love you. _____

I love you. _____

I love you. _____

I love you. _____

I love you. _____

I love you. _____

I love you. _____

I love you. _____

I love you. _____

I love you. _____

As the students came to the end of the test, I could tell by the look on their faces that I had found the perfect parting memory for us. José was sitting in the middle row, the middle seat, as I quietly walked the rows during the test. When I came up behind him, I looked down at his paper and saw that he had written:

> Yo sé.
>
> Yo sé.
>
> Yo sé.
>
> Yo sé.
>
> Yo sé.
>
> Yo sé.
>
> Yo sé.
>
> Yo sé.
>
> Yo sé.
>
> Yo sé.
>
> Yo sé.
>
> Yo sé.
>
> Yo sé.
>
> Yo sé.
>
> Yo sé.
>
> Yo sé.
>
> Yo sé.

Yo sé in English means, "I know." From that moment on I have understood the importance of the teachable heart. José had one; he learned not only what was taught, but much more. And, along the way he taught us all.

Cummins

Jim Cummins's concept of empowerment (1989), which has been used and abused by many, still focuses us on the primacy of power in educational and societal issues. Cummins has taught us that unless we ourselves are empowered, we cannot be involved with any other processes of empowerment. To be voiceless is to be powerless. If we view ourselves as helpless, we are. We cannot control how others have traditionally perceived us, but we can control how we perceive ourselves. Critical pedagogy empowers our theory and action into a personal praxis that challenges the exclusive membership of the A Team.

Empowerment Framework.   Schools often ask: What can we do? I feel Cummins's framework is vastly underrated and underused. Everyone talks about it as a marvelous theoretical construct, but very few do it. I suggest that it is highly doable — tomorrow! It doesn't cost anything; you won't need a mandate; you won't need a committee, nor another spiral notebook for your shelf. Just do it.

The beauty of this model is that it is highly adaptable in any context. As seen in Figure 3.4, Cummins provides guidelines along a powerful path of intervention. It is not a prescribed recipe. Teachers and learners need to bring their knowledge and experience to the model and adapt it to fit their own particular context. Schools and communities can begin the dialogue by examining their own perspectives on Cummins's framework. The following questions, which are all based on Cummins's four areas of the empowerment model, can be used for teachers, students, administrators, and/or com-

FIGURE 3.4   Framework for intervention

SOURCE: From *Empowering Minority Students*, by J. Cummins, 1989, Sacramento: California Association for Bilingual Education. Copyright 1989 by the California Association for Bilingual Education. Reprinted by permission.

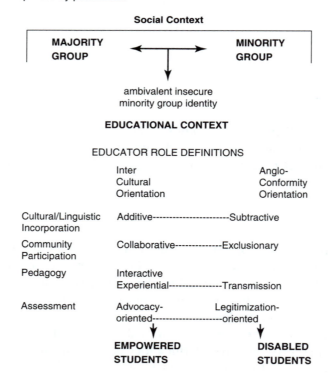

munity members. All you need to do is bring the community together and let the dialogue begin.

1. *Cultural and linguistic incorporation:* Is our theory and practice additive or subtractive? Why? What does that mean? How can we learn? Are all students encouraged to keep their family's culture and to learn more about other cultures, also. What does multicultural mean? What does it mean to me? In what ways do we show respect for all cultures and languages? Do kids come into our schools speaking more than one language and leave 12 years later speaking only one? Why? Does our practice reflect our theory?

2. *Community participation:* Do all families feel included in the school processes? Who does? Who doesn't? How could we learn what families really feel about their inclusion or exclusion? What specific collaborative processes do we have? Who comes? Who doesn't come? Why?

3. *Pedagogy:* What does pedagogy mean? How can we learn? What type do we believe in? Why? Are those beliefs turned into behaviors in our classrooms? How? Do the students really get to interact and experience their own generation of knowledge, or are they just memorizing facts that may soon be dated? What can we do?

4. *Assessment of programs:* When we talk about the programs in our schools, do we find ourselves legitimizing or advocating? What is the difference? How can we learn? What specific programs make me feel like advocating? Why? We always assess our students, but do we ever assess our own role in our local education? Should we? How? Why?

This process of reflection and action leads to empowerment. My only cautionary note for those who plan to examine critically Cummins' empowerment framework is: Allow plenty of time and be supportive of each other and the process. This is not a three-hour in-service. Allow at least a year for the reflective phase and another year for the action. Things will change.

I suspect there are two reasons people don't actually *do* the empowerment framework. First, it seems too simple. How could that possibly work? Don't be fooled. The empowerment framework is not simple, nor is it simplistic. Its merit lies in the fact that it is grounded in highly complex theory and, at the same time, provides a clear picture of action. The four components force us all to confront ourselves as educators and to take the responsibility for our own educational actions. The second reason I think people tend to overlook this framework is because of the connotations of elite jargon that have developed around the "e" word. Okay, I'll say it, "Empower-

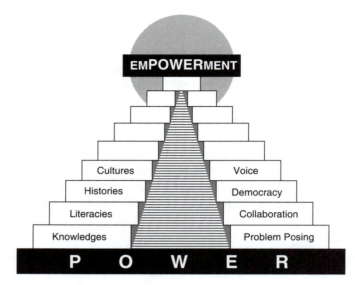

FIGURE 3.5   Putting the power back in emPOWERment

ment. Empowerment. Empowerment." Power is not something to be trivialized. I suggest that we put the power back in empowerment, as demonstrated in Figure 3.5. Jim has joined with Tove to say clearly: "Power is, after all, what it is all about" (Skutnabb-Kangas & Cummins, 1988, p. 390).

The meaning of empowerment is not fixed; it is constantly emerging and redefining itself; its definition is daily informed by teachers and students as they explore its boundaries. However, the primacy of empowerment is power.

In the same way that Peter McLaren has consistently warned us of the insidious danger of critical pedagogy being reduced to nothing more than banal liberal education, Jim Cummins has warned us of the abuse of multicultural education as it becomes nothing more than celebrations of festivals and foods. I far prefer the directness of Cummins's "antiracist; antisexist; anticlassist" education, which forces all educators to confront the real issues of our own involvement in the hidden (and not so hidden) processes of institutionalized racism.

Collaborative and Coercive Relations of Power.   Cummins has continued to expand his ideas of power and empowerment with his concepts of coercive relations of power and collaborative relations of power (Cummins, 1994). We all have experienced coercive relations of power in which it is assumed there is a limited amount of power; power is fixed and subtractive. If one person gets more, the fear is that someone else must get less. These assumptions are nonsense. Power and problems have something in common: there is enough for us all. I have noticed that every time I mention this to a group of educators, there is always a knowing smile of understanding upon hearing that specific language. Well, let me be precise: most smile, a few squirm. What does that tell me? Who smiles? And who squirms? I think you know the answers to these questions.

When you have worked in a coercive environment, how did you feel? Were you effective? Productive? Not me. When I am in coercive environments, I do less, and I do it with anger. Collaborative relations of power assume that power is infinite; it grows and generates during collaborative interactions. When I have been in an environment of collaborative relations of power, I do more, better. The trick for teachers is to have the courage to negotiate their own power even when they are within the context of coercive relations of power.

Krashen

The Idea Generator.   If we teach well, students will eventually quit listening to us. I'm sure he didn't mean to teach that to me, but that is what I have learned! One of Stephen Krashen's best ideas is the Idea Generator. I first heard him talk about it when I was trying to write a grant for a school district. The Idea Generator (Krashen, 1994) is originally based on early cognitive psychology (Wallas, 1926). Krashen also credits parts of the idea to Frank Smith. According to this model, we go through five stages in thinking and generating new ideas.

1. *Gathering information:* I had been reading old grants and worrying.
2. *Preparing ideas:* I began to doodle with words and ideas. I continued to worry.
3. *Incubation:* As I rode my bike to the schools, I asked myself questions and tried to answer them.
4. *Illumination:* When Krashen started to talk, he must have said something that triggered the illumination phase: "Eureka!" I started to write on the yellow legal pad while Krashen continued his lecture. I did not hear another word he said. I quit worrying. I started producing.
5. *Verification:* After my fragile, delicate, baby, tiny ideas were now on yellow legal pad, I rewrote them into the computer. I noticed they started to make more sense. I rewrote again and understood even better. Finally, the district grant-writing committee helped me to verify, affirm, and rewrite my ideas. We mailed the grant.

Some would ask why Krashen is a critical pedagog. Anytime teachers and learners in classrooms generate ideas based on their own lived experiences and transform their own context, I say this is critical pedagogy in action.

Who Gets Books and Who Doesn't? I know, we are not supposed to say that anyone empowers anyone else. To empower seems like a transitive verb; it sounds as if it ought to take an object. What then does "empowerment" look like? As I have watched Steve Krashen travel around the country, it appears he is doing something that turns theory into practice for many, many people. Teachers get it when he asks, "Who gets books and who doesn't?" This year alone I would need more than two hands to count the number of teachers, whom I personally know, who have gone off to a one-day workshop with Krashen and have returned and begun transforming their classes and schools. These are teachers who have had the long-held and, until recently, unchallenged attitude in their tummies that "this-is-America-give-em-books-in-English." Suddenly, they realize that all kids need to read books in their mother tongue. For example, if this book were written in Russian, would you get it? Would you care? Would you read? By asking this one question, Krashen speaks directly to critical pedagogy and the classroom teacher.

The Benson Kids

Critical pedagogy always begins with questions. In the search for my own unique voice within the framework of critical pedagogy, I asked: "Where in the world does it come from?" These philosophical roots originated in many areas of the world and from multiple voices. These voices of culture, experience, language, knowledge, and power provide us with a foundation for further learning. I have painted a picture of the roots, which extend into south and east. In addition, I have written of critical roots on the North American continent that have touched my life. This picture is not all-inclusive, but my wish is that it is enough to peak your curiosity and make you run, buy, or borrow another book.

However, if you really want to know where I learned about critical pedagogy, it was from those Benson kids. They were really the ones who taught me all of this. The University of Arizona and Texas A&M think that they taught me this, but they only affirmed what the students had taught me. I started out with the intention of teaching the Benson kids how to conjugate verbs; they taught me how to teach. These students challenged all the philosophy and methodology that I had previously been taught. When I read roaring, raging books of theory, I see the faces of the students who taught me.

In the next chapter, I will ask the question: "Critical Pedagogy: How in the World Do You Do It?" I suspect that the following chapter will require all of my courage and most of your patience.

LOOKING AHEAD FOR NEW LEADERS: YOU!

Our future together will need new leaders. What critical leadership qualities do you bring to the future?

NOTES

1. Tracking. For further reading on this subject, read Jeannie Oakes (1985), *Keeping track: How schools structure inequality*. New Haven, CT: Yale University Press. Tracking is also a recurring theme with the marvelous Milwaukee group of teachers and their newsletters, *Rethinking Schools*. (Rethinking Schools, 1001 East Keefe Avenue, Milwaukee, Wisconsin 53212; tel.: 414-964-9646; fax: 414-964-7220.) More recently (1995), *Rethinking Schools*, a book (ISBN 1-56584-215-4), was published by The New Press, New York, NY 10110.

2. For a more thorough discussion of the relationship between Freire and Vygotsky, I encourage you to read Christian Faltis (1990), "Freirian and Vygotskian perspective," *Foreign language annals*, 23(2), 117-126. In this seminal article, Faltis explains that Freire's emphasis on critical reflection and action encourages teachers and students to talk about things that really matter to them. Purposeful social interaction in a classroom will open the door to more language and learning. Vygotsky's legacy of a theoretical framework grounded in the social nature of learning involves the negotiation of meaning through dialogue. When these two perspectives come together, teachers have the opportunity of turning theory into practice on a daily basis with students who are involved with language and learning — thus, with all students!

chapter 4

Critical Pedagogy

How in the World Do You Do It?

Always think about practice.
A fundamental Freirian principle as expressed by Gadotti

THINKING ABOUT PRACTICE

Here I sit thinking about practice. Thinking about what can't be written: How to *do* critical pedagogy. In the previous chapters, we have discussed the meaning and the history of critical pedagogy. In this chapter I will move to a harder question: How in the world do you *do* critical pedagogy? Is there a blueprint? a prescription? a recipe? Of course not, which will make writing this chapter fairly problematic. This must be how Mem Fox (1993) felt when she wrote about trying to teach what can't be taught. I am writing about what can't be written. I doubt I can teach someone how to *do* critical pedagogy. We do not *do* critical pedagogy; we *live* it.

Yeahbut, How?

However, my view of *living* critical pedagogy is balanced by the persistent voice of Dawn Wink, who keeps rolling her eyes and saying:

> *"Yeahbut,* how, *Mom?"*

If you are one of the practitioners, who constantly says, "how?" you will be glad to know that I have suffered a lot in the preparation of this chapter. Whenever I try to explain to someone that you don't *do* critical pedagogy, you *live* it, *how* just keeps creeping into the conversation. For example, when I told Dawn about self and social transformation, emancipatory pedagogy, a spirit of inquiry, problem posing, she sighed and asked, "How?" When I told her to have students interview their parents, she queried, "Yeah but, what about the parents who question me because my students don't get dittos like the other kids?" When I told her to record her student-generated questions on the board, she came home and asked, "Okay, now I have 30 student-generated questions on the board, now what?"

The fact is that I love to play with the dialectic of *living* or *doing* critical pedagogy. The fact is that Dawn Wink is not as charmed with this as I am. So, for all the *Dawn Winks*, I hesitatingly offer these guidelines for *doing* critical pedagogy. I encourage you to take and shape them to fit the needs of your students. All the following guidelines are based on Paulo Freire's concept of problem posing: to name, to reflect critically, and to act.

The practitioners' voice in critical pedagogy must be as strong as the theorists' voice. It is always easier to state a theoretical concept than it is to live it with 30 or 40 students every day. The voice of critical pedagogy must flow in both directions. This ongoing dialogue with Dawn has offered me the opportunity to relearn and unlearn as her practice informs my theory and my theory informs her practice.

Jonathan: A Reflection

How to *do* critical pedagogy? Let's reflect together. Why in the world did I begin a book about critical pedagogy with a story about Jonathan? Why is it that I could learn so much about teaching and learning from him? Was I *doing* critical pedagogy? Problem posing is central in critical pedagogy; what does problem posing have to do with Jonathan?

Problem Posing

> to name
> to reflect critically
> to act

Paulo Freire has taught that to teach and learn critically we can follow this straightforward guideline: to name, to reflect critically, to act. I have found this to be extremely effective in my own teaching and learning. However, I also have discovered that sometimes educators are *doing/living* this framework without realizing it. I also have discovered that when we ask teachers/learners *to name* the problem, they respond, "What?" Sometimes, I suspect that when I ask students *to name*, they think that I talk funny. When we *name* a problem, a situation, we are doing nothing more than conceptualizing critically and articulating clearly.

Let's rethink the experiences of Jonathan using this framework as a guide for our own reflection.

To name. In the Jonathan story, *to name* would be to say that he could not decode and encode; he could not read and write, as they have traditionally been defined. In this particular case, it is fairly easy *to name.* Sometimes, it is not so easy *to name* the problem.

To reflect critically. What did I do to reflect critically in this situation? I listened, I watched, I talked, I thought, I read, I called specialists, I tried lots of methods, I loved Jon. What did his parents do? All of this and more. In addition, they talked to the teacher (after teacher, after teacher), they listened to specialists, they went to student-study-team meetings, they agonized, they waited, they read and read and read stories to Jon, they provided other avenues of success, and they loved Jon. What did Jonathan do? He tried and tried and tried; and, periodically, he gave up and cried. How do I know all of this? I wrote and reflected and listened and read and wrote some more. For more than six years, the Jonathan files in my computer grew and grew. I had no idea what would happen with all of this.

To act. What did Jonathan's parents do? They enrolled Jon in a program that was expensive and very much the opposite of much of the advice they were receiving; like, from me, for example. I believe critical pedagogy helps us to grow in patience and courage. They had been patient long enough; now, they needed to be courageous. What did I do to act? One week I sat down and opened the Jonathan files and pulled the story together because I saw that we can all learn from his experiences. In this particular case, I am not sure if I wrote the story or if it wrote itself.

During all of this time, did I ever think that I was *doing* critical pedagogy? Never. Not once. Was I doing critical pedagogy? Probably, but I prefer to think that I was simply living my beliefs. I care about Jonathan; I care about his entire family; I care about kids learning to read; I care about teaching and learning. I just had to keep a close eye on all of this. I couldn't stop myself.

Now, here's the point: I believe that many educators are doing the very same thing in their own educational context. Every day with my work with teachers, I observe similar powerful situations. Every night in my graduate classes, I hear incredible stories of teachers and students and families. At the grass roots level, teachers are making a difference in the lives of students. But, I suggest that it is helpful to stop thinking of ourselves as just methodologists. We are more than that: Critical pedagogy enables us to understand that we also are professionals and intellectuals who have the power to take part actively in self and social transformation. Critical pedagogy makes us keep on keeping on.

Sometimes when we try to define problem posing it can be helpful to reflect on our own teaching and learning. Terry captures the meaning of problem posing by thinking of her own experiences:

> *Problem posing always makes me think of liberation. If the purpose of education truly is human liberation, then why are we always trying to box in ideas? We are always trying to fit powerful ideas into a scope and sequence, a curriculum, a skill continuum, or another district-mandated process. Problem posing cannot be confined to these boxes. When I think of liberated people, I think of Maya Angelou who flies above all the boxes that others have created. I think of my high school literature teacher, Miss Johnson. In her class, we lived problem posing every day, and we didn't even know it. She opened the world for us; she hated syllabi. Her enthusiasm ignited our journeys of learning. We had tons of books of all kinds in her class, and we had time to read whatever we chose. We read and talked and discussed and wrote. And, we created a community in the process.*
>
> *Miss Johnson listened to our hidden voices. She taught us to listen to each other. We learned that any problem could have many solutions.*
>
> *She taught us to name; to reflect critically; and to act. I particularly remember one of the problems we posed.*
>
>> To name. *This was during the sixties, and the girls were not allowed to wear pants to school. We were angry about this. We used to go to her room and talk about it. In her class, we knew we could name anything we wanted. We just didn't know that we were naming!*
>>
>> To reflect critically. *We spent many lunch periods in her*

classroom talking about our anger. She would listen to each of us. If it mattered to us, it mattered to her.

To act. *After considering several options, we devised a plan that was very radical in those days. We wrote letters and carried them to the student council, the administration, and the school board to ask that* girls *be allowed to wear pants to school. I remember the boys on the student council; the men administrators, and the men on the school board saying no: Girls had to wear dresses. However, the year after we graduated, pants were allowed for all students.*

Apparently, I have overlooked a significant event in the histories of women of my age. On the same week that Terry wrote this reflection, another grad student/teacher handed in a splendid timeline that reflected the educational changes from Comenius to Freire. On this timeline she had written: 1966 – *girls* finally were allowed to wear pants to school.

Principles of Problem Posing

Teachers and Learners:

trust each other;

believe that their involvement will matter;

understand resistance and institutional barriers to change;

are aware of their own power and knowledge.

If we look back on Terry's experience, we can see that these principles of problem posing were embedded in this process. For example: The students and teacher trusted each other; they believed they could change the dress code; they knew the student council members, the administrators, and school board would probably say no initially; and, they had a sense that they could make a difference because, after all, the dress code did affect their lives every day. It had very little effect on those who had created the rule. Maybe perseverance should be another principle of problem posing.

The Teacher's Role in Problem Posing

> to create a safe place for it to happen;
> to ask hard questions for the students' musing;
> to assist students with codification.

Miss Johnson opened her classroom during lunch and after school. Terry and her friends knew they were welcome. As the *girls* talked, Miss Johnson periodically would ask questions that they had never considered. For example, who made this rule about pants? Miss Johnson had suggested to the girls that they write letters with their concerns; she had led them into the act of codification. As I have written previously, codification is the problem represented in some format. What might this codification look like? It can be captured in clay, in paint, in chalk, in pencil, in music, in any art form. In the process of problem posing, the learners capture their feelings and meanings about a problem.

Freeman and Freeman (1992) have clarified problem posing for many teachers whom I know. Their codification model is grounded in the work of Freire and is amplified for teachers' ease in implementation. It has been my experience that many teachers are ready to problem pose; however, it is challenging, and they often are confused about codification. Freeman and Freeman offer the following model of codification:

- The code is a whole story, picture, or film.
- The code is based on the learners' lives.
- Learners identify and solve real-life problems.
- Learners work cooperatively to solve community problems.
- The goal is literacy for the learners.
- The goal is for teachers and students to empower themselves.

Freeman and Freeman (1992) extend their codification processes to their version of problem posing in which they offer six phases. Adapting their model, I offer the following four phases of problem posing.

1. *Begin with the student's own experience.* In schools, we are so focused on *doing*, on *covering* that we don't take time to think; to

reflect; to muse. My sense is that we, as teachers, have failed our students by not taking the time to encourage students to reflect quietly on their lived experiences. Yes, learning can take place in noisy, interactive classrooms. Learning also can take place when we silently reflect. The only thing teachers hate more than noise is silence, I have often heard Yetta Goodman, who teaches at the University of Arizona, say. She is right.

2. *Identify, investigate, pose a problem within your own life*. At this point, teachers need to let go of control; student-centered learning is about to begin. Students generate knowledge about the problem; they brainstorm where, when, and how they can learn more about it. Students set out to learn what they want to know. They codify ideas; they interview experts in the community; they find information in the library, through technology, from any resource with accessible information. Teachers can facilitate this process by helping students find language to conceptualize and articulate their thoughts. Teachers ask leading questions about resources for more learning and possible connections to students' lives. Teachers stay out of the way.

3. *Solve the problem together*. After conceptualizing, articulating, and researching the problem, learners work together to solve the problem.

4. *Action*. Learners make a plan and act on it. Learners discover that their learning and their involvement really does matter. Learners are empowered by their own learning and action. They realize that their social interaction can lead to self and social transformation.

Problem posing always ends with action. Once the learners have identified and captured (named) their concern, they take action; find solutions; extend the dialogue of the classroom to the real world. What might this action look like? It can be a letter to the editor, governor, legislators, or presidents; interviewing others; oral histories; meetings with policy-making committees; cleaning up a community; beginning an environmental, social, cultural, or political action group.

Problem posing takes place when people begin with a spirit of inquiry and questioning of situations that directly affects their own lives. Problem posing ends with actions and transformation. Problem posing begins again. Goal: literacy and knowledge. Knowledge is generative. We use language to generate our own knowledge. Social interaction leads to self and social transformation.

HISTORY AND HOW-TO

History sheds light on why we do what we do. We are a reflection of all that has gone before us; we are indebted to the people and the ideas that have preceded us. When I started teaching in 1966, the world was a very different place. I do things very differently in my classes now, but I know that what I do in classes every day is touched by all the teaching, learning, and believing that has preceded me. Looking back historically can illuminate our present as we run to catch the future. In what follows, we will examine three approaches that represent unique educational beliefs and behaviors.

Transmission Model

The teacher is standing in front of the classroom, and the students are at their seats, which are in rows. They listen to what she says and write it down in their notebooks.

"A carrot is a root. We eat many roots. It is orange, and it is good for you. Other roots we eat are onions, beets, jicama, potatoes. Class, are you writing everything that I tell you? Today I will classify plants to those you can eat and those you can't. Make two columns on your paper and be sure to get every word I say for your homework. You will have a test on these exact words tomorrow. Who can name some other roots that we eat?"

I suspect that every one of us has had a similar experience. Were you taught this way? Do you teach this way? Why? For centuries, the vision of the teacher in front of the class pouring knowledge into students heads guided the image of pedagogy. In this instructional model, the teacher has the knowledge, and the students receive that knowledge. The teacher's job is to transmit knowledge. The teacher controls who knows what; power has always been a part of pedagogy.

I began my career in much the same way; I taught the way I was taught. In fact, I was a true eight-year-old direct instruction specialist, maybe even a zealot. I made my girlfriends sit on the basement steps, and I stood on the cement floor below, and I taught. Oh, did I teach! I spoke, they listened. I had the knowledge in my head, and all I had to do was transmit it to them. What power. I could control their knowledge. For evaluation, they had to give it back to me exactly the way I gave it to them. Why in the world did they ever come to play with me? Fortunately, since the days of stair-step pedagogy, we have learned a lot about teaching and learning, not to mention the fact that the world has changed, too. Politically, economically, scientifically, ecologically, culturally, demographically, those days are gone. That was then; this is now.

Today, we have more complex understandings of who students are and how they learn. This new knowledge has raised questions about the traditional way of transmitting previous knowledge. Educators and researchers increasingly recognize the role students play in constructing knowledge and accessing new knowledge. The teacher-directed lesson too often lacks opportunities for students to interact with one another and with the ideas that they are studying. In addition, in linguistically diverse classrooms, the teacher-directed lesson is often incomprehensible to students who are still learning English. We can't learn what we don't understand.

To address these problems, more and more educators focus their pedagogy on discovery, exploration, and inquiry. While intrigued by these ideas, many teachers find themselves at a loss in terms of how to structure these kinds of learning experiences in their crowded classrooms.

Generative Model

Now, imagine a classroom with small groups of students clustered around various learning centers. At each center students are exploring the properties of edible roots. One group is cutting a potato, a carrot, and an onion and dropping iodine on the pieces to see if they contain starch. Another group is sorting through an array of vegetables to determine which are edible roots. At still a third center, a group is setting up jars to sprout potatoes. The teacher moves around the room, quietly observes, and periodically interacts with various groups.

The teacher moves to the group that has jars for sprouting potatoes. "I see your group has used different amounts of water in your jars. Can you predict which potato will sprout first? Why?"

The generative model maintains that students must actively engage in their learning process. Learning is not passive. Students generate meaning as they integrate new ideas and previous knowledge. Simply put, students are participants in their own learning. The teacher's job is to structure and guide classroom experiences that will lead to student learning. In the following classroom scene, the teacher uses a structured cooperative approach to guide her teaching and to encourage the students to generate knowledge.

It is time for science, and Mrs. Esperanza's bilingual classroom looks and sounds very different from the other fourth-grade classrooms at Beadle School. It is distinguished not just by the level of activity and movement, but by the volume and variety of sounds emanating from it. On the board are three questions:

What is sound?
What makes a sound's pitch high or low?
How does sound travel?

Students are working in groups of four at different learning center activities. Each center has a task card in both Spanish and English. At one center students have arranged a series of bottles with different water levels in them. They are blowing into the bottles to create different pitched sounds. If you listened closely, you would hear a tune faintly reminiscent of "De Colores" emanating from this corner of the room. In another center students have made simple telephones using paper cups attached by long strings. They are having a heated argument over whether the large or the small cups make a better receiver. Several groups appear to be making musical instruments. One group wraps rubber bands around cardboard boxes, while another is making kazoos using straws of different lengths. You notice several students in a corner of the room humming intently with their hands on their throats.

Students wear badges identifying their group role and around the room you note colorful signs outlining different student roles and responsibilities. The facilitator is responsible to make sure that everyone understands the task, and is the only one who can call the teacher; the checker makes sure everyone gets the help they need on worksheets; the materials manager organizes the setup and cleanup process, while reporters will eventually report back to the whole class on the results of the group activity. A large blue poster states, "You have the right to ask for help and the duty to give help."

In front of the room is a poster with a list of skills, abilities, or knowledge bases that appear to be highly relevant for these tasks: observing accurately, analysis of a problem, design and construction of musical instruments, creativity, hearing pitch, creating melody, and knowing musical notation. Above the poster is a sign reading, "No one has all of the necessary abilities; everyone has some of the abilities" (Wink & Swanson, 1993).

Learning and Cooperating.   Mrs. Esperanza's classroom is using a form of cooperative learning designed to develop higher order thinking skills in heterogeneous classrooms that evolved from the Program for Complex Instruction at Stanford University. This type of instruction rests on three central tenets: a changed curriculum, new roles for the teacher and the students, and ensuring access for all students. These structured cooperative processes foster the development of higher order thinking skills through group work activities organized around a central theme. The tasks are open-ended, requiring students to work interdependently to problem solve. Most importantly, the curriculum is multiple ability. The tasks require a wide array of different kinds of intellectual abilities so that children from diverse backgrounds and different levels of academic proficiency can make meaningful contributions to the group task.

Often children with limited school background, or who do not yet speak English, are perceived by their peers as less competent. As a consequence, they are given less opportunity to participate, and they learn less. To ensure equal access to learning, Mrs. Esperanza knows she must address these status problems. Teachers using complex instruction use two "status treatments" (the multiple abilities treatment and the assignment of competence) to change students' perceptions concerning what it means to be smart, and to convince them that each student has important intellectual contributions to make to the multiple ability task (Wink & Swanson, 1993).

Cooperative learning, with all its multiple forms and varieties, has much to offer any classroom. Depending on the particular objective of the learning activity and the needs of the students, it can work very effectively to break down social barriers and motivate learners. As with all good learning and teaching, it is not the only way, but certainly a very good way.

Tribes, a cooperative learning model developed by Jeanne Gibbs (1994) focuses on inclusion, participation, and community. Gibbs believes that trust is fundamental to building a cohesive group; therefore, students are assured they will be in a group with at least one person of their choosing. Kagan (1990) emphasizes a structured approach that fosters interdependence and intergroup relationships. Johnson and Johnson (1987) have focused on the conditions that improve cooperative learning activities. Both their model and that of Kagan tend to be curriculum-free and can be applied in various contexts. Slavin (1985) has developed a model that is curriculum-specific but always focuses on the inherent nature of cooperation. The one thing I have learned about cooperative learning is that it is not just a bunch of kids sitting in groups and talking! Each of the models offers far more structure, complexity, and potential!

When cooperative structures are implemented with care and knowledge, student groups manage themselves, and Mrs. Esperanza now has the time to observe groups, provide specific feedback, ask questions designed to foster critical reflection, and focus on the dynamics of power within groups that can lead to unequal participation among group members.

However, as we can learn from the next example, it is often difficult to change from a tradition of transmission to a more generative form of learning. Ken, a beginning teacher, shares his critical reflection with us:

> *The first-grade students were observing the wax worms. They were to write, draw, and classify their observations. They were mesmerized by the worms and were very excited and focused on their assignments. They were talking, and writing, and drawing, and observing. In short, they were doing all that I had been taught in my teacher preparation program. However, I was having difficulty with the noise. It was like I was having this inner conflict within myself. It was a contradiction. It was change. It was hard. Intellectually, I knew this was a hands-on, interactive process that generates meaningful learning, but my past experience made me want a quiet class with students seated in clean rows. As the children worked and learned and loved it, I began to write in my journal why I was so uncomfortable with the loud noise. I grew up with the transmission or behaviorist educational theory. I had been socialized to think this was the only and the best way. I realized that I was uncomfortable because I was experiencing a contradiction of learning theories and practices. My reflection made me begin to rethink some of my educational experiences. I guess I am relearning and unlearning, not only from theory, but also from the practice of the classroom.*

Tanya is another beginning teacher who is reflecting critically on her own learning and that of her students, the majority of whom are ethnic minorities — which, of course, makes them the majority in her own classroom. Her continual theory building and the daily experiences with the students is a powerful pedagogical process for Tanya. She writes:

When I went to school, we sat in individual desks — in rows — and the teacher told us what we needed to know; there was no need for inquiry or for us to interact with each other and the context. I think of how many times I have studied for tests — even at the college level — with no understanding of the material, yet I carefully memorized the notes, texts, and buzz words and quoted back what the teacher had told us.

In fact, I have only begun to understand some math concepts (such as where those zeros come from in multiplication!) now that I am teaching in math in a meaningful way. It seems that many teachers and parents refuse to accept any other method of learning, except the way they were taught. Something that is very new for me is that students who come from nondominant cultures and languages need to engage in meaningful experiences and to interact with authentic materials. As I watch the students in my classes, I can see that it just makes so much sense.

Now, I am learning by reflecting on my own experiences and those of the students that almost everything memorized will soon be forgotten unless the students really find it meaningful. I used to believe in drill, drill, drill. As educators, we have an awesome responsibility to see that real learning is taking place in our classrooms.

Transformative Model

Now, let's visit another classroom that is also studying carrots, and onions, and roots. The educational model that is being used in the following classroom is historically rooted in the transmission and generative models. However, this model reflects, not only the changing world, but also our more complex understandings of meaningful teaching and learning. This model reflects today and prepares for tomorrow.

Imagine a classroom where small groups of students are outside working in their garden, which they planted several months ago. The students are digging the potatoes, carrots, and onions and weighing them. Based on their production costs, the students will determine their price per pound later in math class. The group has decided in their class meeting that they will sell a portion of the roots in order to earn money for the scholarships for a field trip. The remainder of the garden vegetables will be donated to the local food kitchen.

In transformative pedagogy, or critical pedagogy, the goal includes generating knowledge, but extends from the classroom to the world. Some would say that this group of students *is doing* critical pedagogy.

What if the subject matter were social studies, and the teacher wanted the students to use their knowledge and abilities to affect society. A large goal indeed!

The Reformation

Seventh-grade students in Mrs. Smith's class are studying the Reformation. While often students find this segment of European history distant and removed from their daily lives, this year the Reformation has taken on a new meaning. Students are studying the Reformation in light of the following question: How does a group or an individual challenge the authority of institutions? This is a question of consummate interest for seventh graders!

After providing background information on the historical and political context of the Reformation, Mrs. Smith has the students work in groups to explore different facets of this turbulent time. Some are reading about Martin Luther and designing a skit to show how he challenged the authority of the Pope; another group is examining diagrams of the first printing press and building a model printing press, while still others are discussing political cartoons from the Reformation.

The group studying political cartoons seems particularly intense. After studying a number of cartoons criticizing the Pope for selling indulgences, they are asked to create their own political cartoon, which would challenge the authority of a current institution. The students discuss our society's institutions and those practices that they would call into question. The discussion is intense as the topic is not light. The students in this ethnically diverse school have been following the Rodney King beating case closely. They decide to design a cartoon that questions the authority of the police and the legal system, which had, at that point in time, just acquitted the officers of beating Rodney King. They drew a white policeman, holding a gun and standing on top of a black man. The policeman is saying, "We stand on top of our work," and the black man on the ground replies, "You can say that again."

It was a powerful and troubling cartoon and an articulate testimony to the students' distress and anger. It conveyed the abstract ideas of both authority and oppression and was a searing indictment of our legal institutions. It was the beginning of social action.

The transformative lesson distinguishes itself in two ways from the generative mode. First, it is designed so the students act upon and use their generated knowledge for self and social transformation. The socially constructed knowledge of the classroom is to be applied in the social context of life. Second, this lesson design is inherently grounded in democratic principles.

Democracy is at the heart of the transformative lesson. While schooling in the United States has historically prided itself on teaching democratic principles, how many schools are truly democratic? If you would like to explore this question, the next time you are with a group of teachers, initiate a discussion of democracy. It's all the rage. Everyone is for it. Then ask them if they work in a democratic school. I have done this on multiple occasions in large staff-development groups with many teachers. I consistently have been amazed at the level of cynicism of teachers when they discuss the lack of democracy in their own schools. It would take more than one hand for me to count the social studies teachers I know who teach democracy but admit they do not live and work in a democratic environment. Ah, these contradictions are confounding! It seems that in schools we teach it well; apparently, we don't live it quite as well.

The philosophy that supports transformative teaching and learning is founded on the principle that theory and practice are joined to form praxis. Not only must democracy be taught, it must be lived within the classroom, the school, and the community. Lesson designs that spring from this philosophical basis seek to break down the harmful forces of marginalization. This model of lesson design seeks to assure all communities of learners' equity and access to both academic resources and power structures of society.

Democracy with Teachers

Recently, I witnessed a marvelous example of democracy in action—although the word was never mentioned. Mark is a principal at a school that has a Latino American enrollment of 80 percent.

At this school as in many others, the "minority" is the "majority." Therefore, if minority means less (in numbers), and majority means more (in numbers), I could no longer say the Latino students are the minority. However, I have noticed that sometimes schools with a high enrollment of Latino Americans, African Americans, or Asian Americans are often called minority schools.

This always makes me wonder what minority now means. Could it be that minority means less, and majority means more in hidden terms of value, status, prestige, power? Are we in schools unconsciously assigning value to one group of students and not another. As the world changes, our language must reflect these changes.

Mark, and several teachers in the district, had gone to an intensive workshop of labor relations sponsored by a nonprofit corporation that works to improve the relationship between districts and unions. Together the administrators and teachers had discussed the complex issues of consensus building, management styles, top-down and bottom-up administrative processes, etc. The week Mark returned to his school, a regularly scheduled faculty meeting was planned.

Traditionally, Mark had always prepared the agenda (mostly by himself) prior to the meetings. The established pattern was for Mark to speak and the teachers to listen. Teachers left their classrooms to immediately become passive learners. However, at this meeting he and the teachers identified the topics that needed to be discussed, and together they created the agenda. Whereas previously the rules of the meetings were socially assumed based on protocol and imposed from the top down, now the teachers and administrators were jointly creating their own educational process. The emphasis had shifted from product to process.

The transformative model of lesson design is just another name for critical pedagogy. In this case the teacher and the students are not only *doing* critical pedagogy, they are *living* critical pedagogy. The fundamental belief that drives these classroom behaviors is that we must act; we must relate our teaching and learning to real life; we must connect our teaching and learning with our communities; we always try to learn and teach so that we grow and so that students' lives are improved, or for self and social transformation.

In the traditional classroom, instruction outcomes are often quite narrow and specific (memorized concepts, vocabulary, and skills); in the transformational model, student outcomes are as complex as the complexities of our diverse society. The problems students study and the range of possible solutions reflect the dilemmas of the larger society, and the complexity of society is mirrored in both the instructional strategies and content of classroom discourse.

This new approach to teaching and learning challenges teachers to have complex pedagogical skills. The practices of teachers must be informed by new theories of unrestricted human development, inclusion, multiple voices, relationships, and everyone's everyday life (García, 1993, p. 4). Traditionally, the teacher spoke, and the students listened. In the transformational model, teachers are challenged to expand the boundaries of classroom discourse. What the students say and feel matters. Discourse is based on equity, and seeks to empower the voice of the most disenfranchised students. Teachers are called upon to understand that language is a powerful tool for the creation of knowledge and justice.[1]

HOW-NOT-TO

Sometimes children are unconsciously trained to think of themselves as less or as more. Sometimes, little girls think they can *do* less than little boys; brown children think they can *do* less than white children; poor children think they can *do* less than rich children. Not only do they think they can *do* less; sometimes they feel they *are* less. I believe this is what Paulo Freire is talking about in *Literacy: Reading the Word and the World*. Even before children are reading words, they are reading us very well. They are reading the world when they walk outside their doors and meet us on the streets, on the buses, in the stores. They *get* the hidden messages we are sending even when we don't realize we are sending messages. Students are socialized by

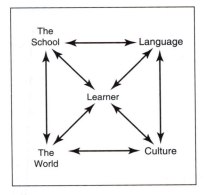

FIGURE 4.1 Student in the center

the greater context; they are led to think in a certain way just because of what they see and hear in their environment. We do not live in a vacuum. Schools do not operate in isolation. All that goes on around us sends messages to us, and each of us responds in various ways. The influences flow in both directions (Cortés, 1986) as can be seen in Figure 4.1. The story of Pablo with the coat over his head demonstrates this interactive nature of the social-cultural context. Pablo is just one example. Sometimes we in schools have a tendency to look only at the student, and even to blame the student, instead of seeing the larger world. Context. Context. Context. I will never forget when I first understood this. A seventh-grade boy, Jim, had been misbehaving in my class. I called his mother to come and visit with Jim and me. When she finished with the two of us, I never *ever* saw him in the same way. I had been introduced to his world. I understood a little better how students read their world and respond to their world.

Oftentimes the language we use and the ideas we (consciously or unconsciously) believe lead little boys and girls to believe that boys are more valuable; white is more valuable; rich is more valuable. I grew up believing that I could only be a nurse, a secretary, or a teacher. I read my world, and I understood my options. Does this still exist in more hidden ways?

> *A mother walked into a classroom with her two daughters*
> *trailing behind her. She was there to pick up her son after school.*
> *"When my son was born, there was much rejoicing!" the mother*
> *proudly said to the teacher. The teacher said nothing but glanced at*
> *the two daughters who stood slightly behind their mother. They both*
> *lowered their heads in silence as they read their world.*

These words are sending powerful messages to these two daughters. They are reading their world and learning that their brother has more value.

These two little girls really believe that their brother is *more*, and they are *less*. This family comes from a country where young women are chosen to be a wife by the family of the future husband. In that culture, wives traditionally have been placed on a lower level of status within the community; at least, that is the perspective of the dominant culture in the United States. However, I have had multiple experiences with women from that particular culture who have explained to me that they are convinced there is more gender biasing in the United States than in the country of their birth. Oh, these contradictions that are a part of our educational spaces. My perspective could be: No, they are wrong, and I am right. More gender biasing obviously exists in their culture. However, I have never been there, so how in the world would I know?! Once again, I find that relearning and unlearning make me uncomfortable at times.

The world (that would include each of us) sends troubling messages every day to kids. They get it. They hear it. They read their world very well.

TEACHER: Class, now that we have finished our social studies units on the presidents of the United States, I would like to know what you would do if you were the president.

BOY #1: Oh, I would . . .

BOY #2: And, I would . . .

TEACHER: Great. Susan, what would you do if you were president?

BOY #1: She can't be the president, only his wife.

TEACHER: Why do you believe that Susan can only be the wife?

How did this little boy learn that Susan can only be the wife? And, what does *only* mean here. Words matter. Has this little boy learned that being a wife is, somehow, less?

Critical pedagogy always begins with questions, and this teacher is asking a great question. Critical pedagogy is driven by a powerful spirit of inquiry — reflective inquiry into the messages we might be sending; reflective inquiry into how we might do things better. We, as learners, are schooled to think our job is to acquire information, but critical pedagogy forces us to inquire into our questions and answers. Critical pedagogy encourages us to examine why boys believe their classmates can *only* be presidents' wives. This boy has built his theory on history, and now his teacher is asking him to inquire into his history.

In the study of critical pedagogy, we are attracted to questions and contradictions in our own educational lives. We seek to understand the opposites we experience in our own lives. This spirit of inquiry leads us to problem pose, and problem posing leads us to try to improve, not only our life, but the lives of those around us. Problem posing pushes us to reexamine some of our own *how-not-to's* and those of others.

The words and ideas of learning and relearning are not just for the classroom — they are for living in real life. In critical pedagogy, academic rigor is encouraged and respected, but not just for a spirited dialogue in the class. The words and ideas are meant to help us understand more deeply and live more fully. The words and ideas of critical pedagogy are for improving the quality of teaching and learning in classes and in life.

A colleague of mine is an African American woman. Our lived experiences are vastly different. She is urban; I am rural. She is black; I am white. We each have received very different messages from the world, and we like to compare our contrasting experiences. A small example popped into our conversation a few weeks ago. She was angered because she always has to get out her ID to write a check. I asked her where. She mentioned three places where I also write checks, but have never been asked to show identification. So, we devised a tiny research project: We went shopping to the three places together; we stood in line together; we wrote checks together. Yes, I received the "hello-Dr.-Wink-how-are-you" greeting, and she received the "may-we-see-your-ID" greeting.

The world sends messages to each of us. We, as educators, send messages, too. Some of those messages are very empowering, and some of those messages are very disabling. Previously, in this book I said that all learning is not comfortable. For example, learning the *how-not-to's* of critical pedagogy has not been fun.

Sometimes teachers, and not students, are on the receiving end of the *how-not-to's* of critical pedagogy. In fact, there are many ways to hurt a teacher, and those of us who have worked in schools for many years, finally have come to understand this. Sometimes, teachers are given difficult assignments or placements (1) as retaliation, or (2) as an attempt to encourage them to leave. I did not like learning this when I was teaching in public schools. But, I finally figured out that it really does happen. Sometimes, these processes even become institutionalized, so they are difficult to see. For example, in one district I know, teachers resist being placed in the "trash" track. This raises lots of very difficult questions that can only be answered by looking critically at the entire context. What is the "trash" track, you ask? It is the "track" that has been (consciously or unconsciously) assigned less status and power and prestige. I know many teachers in this district who resist ever being placed on this track. I know teachers on this track who feel "less." Who are the students who are placed in this track? You already know the answer: students from lower socioeconomic communities and ethnic minorities. I have not liked learning this. As I write the painful parts of this book, a certain rhythm often pounds through my head;

it is almost like the beat of a drum or a mantra. Race, class, gender. Race, class, gender. Race, class, gender. I find as I reflect critically on educational processes, which often are supported and maintained by people (and even people I like), these three words keep popping into my head.

Another example of being aware of assigning status and power to one group and not another was relayed to me by a friend in a university in another state. We were discussing the call for proposals for a national conference. We were studying the various strands or emphases for our proposal submission. We both agreed that the ideas we wanted to share would be appropriate for the multicultural strand. Later, at his institution, he was encouraged by others on the faculty not to submit to that particular strand, as not enough people who really mattered would attend those sessions. It would be better to reframe the ideas to fit into a more mainstream strand. In this case, critical pedagogy enabled me to see that multiculturalism had just been marginalized.

SO HOW? LESSON DESIGN MODELS FOR CRITICAL PEDAGOGY

In transformative education, the spirit of inquiry leads the search for meaning. Students need to have classrooms in which they are safe to take risks. In this pedagogical model, teachers shift from control of knowledge to creation of processes whereby students take ownership of their learning and take risks to understand and apply their knowledge. Students and teachers come to realize that their actions can make a difference. All the following inquiry-based approaches are various ways of problem posing, which is at the very heart of transformative teaching and learning. And, transformative teaching and learning is the heart and soul of *doing* critical pedagogy.

Four Phases #1

Dialogue, or talk seriously with someone;

Dialectic, or try to understand other ways of understanding;

Reflection, or think hard and muse a lot;

Action, or do something about your beliefs.

In the first stage of the lesson, teacher and students *dialogue*. They choose and articulate the idea to be studied. The content of the lesson may be student generated; it may spring from a story they are reading, or it may reflect a concept the students are currently studying. The idea to be learned is connected to their prior knowledge, and students are encouraged to negotiate meaning with their language. When Carmen and Rainey and their co-workers (chapter 2) decided to focus their attention on family involvement at their school, they dialogued first. In fact, they talked and shared their perspectives for several months.

In the *dialectic* stage, the teacher and learners have identified a concept, posed a problem, or articulated an idea to be explored. The teacher facilitates the creation of new knowledge by helping students find language to conceptualize and articulate the various parts, multiple facets, variables, contradictions, pros and the cons. Opposing views are explored to establish a more complex understanding of the whole idea. When Carmen and Rainey began their dialogue, a dialectic naturally emerged as these two teachers had lived vastly different lives; their experiences were opposite on many levels; divergent perspectives were explored at length between the two of them and with their colleagues.

Reflection follows. Taking time to think is good. After conceptualizing and articulating the problem, learners take time for new ideas to incubate and to create patterns and connections. Reflection may involve the silence of independent musings or the noise of working together to solve the problems. The reflections of Rainey were particularly poignant as her dialogue with Carmen forced her to face some of her long-held assumptions — something that is never easy for any of us.

In the final stage, the learners apply their knowledge through *action*. Learners become empowered as they realize that their action can lead to self and social transformation. In this case, Carmen, Rainey, and their colleagues visited the families in their own homes before they invited them to come to the first meeting at the school.

Four Phases #2

A second four-phases process that you might want to try is something I learned while learning with the Benson kids. I clearly remember the day I was standing in front of them, wondering what we would do to survive the initial week together. It suddenly came to me as I looked at all their faces: Everyone in this room can *think*. It seems too simple, but for me at that time, it was pure empowerment. Once I realized that everyone could *think*, I felt like we could do anything. When I suddenly grasped that all the students could think, I immediately knew that I could teach. What a relief! All I had to do is start with what the students know. From that day on, I have carried this magic lesson plan around with me to various places. I have used it with all ages and have found it to be simple and effective.

```
Think
Talk
Write — Read
Do
```

First, start with what the learners are *thinking* about. Ask them. This is how we bring in the world and the knowledge of the learners. This is how we validate their lived experiences. This is how we start where the learners are starting. This is how we begin to let go of control and move from teacher-centered learning to student-centered learning. For example, the "I love you" in multiple languages lesson began when one student was thinking: how do I say I love you in Spanish? in German? in French?

Second, ask them to *talk* about what they know. As we learned from Vygotsky, learning is a very social process. We need to talk to learn. Dialogue is central to critical teaching and learning. The teacher's role is to ask meaningful questions and invite the learners to share their thoughts and knowledge. In the previous example, the students immediately began to talk about saying "I love you" in Dutch, in Swahili, in Russian, etc., as they named all the languages that popped into their minds.

Third, *write* everything that is said. Well, okay, almost everything. With young children, the teacher records their thoughts; with older learners one of them can be doing this while the teacher is generating questions and responses. Record their thoughts. Use butcher paper, the chalkboard, a transparency, anything you can find. This is how the teacher begins the codification of the learners' knowledge. As the students continued to list languages, we recorded this list on the chalkboard and simultaneously began to construct a large world map on another chalkboard.

Fourth, *read, read, read*. Anything. Where can we all learn more about the subject? Who will read what? Who will interview whom to learn more? This is really just another way of doing teacher research in the class. After the learners and teachers have generated a topic, a problem, a theme, we all go out to learn more. After this initial (and extremely spontaneous and energetic) dialogue, the students created continent team-groups for learning more languages in their continent; they went to the library for maps and books and brainstormed others ways of accessing the information that they wanted.

This process can be done in one hour, in three hours, in a week, etc. The "I love you" lesson continued for several weeks. Whatever your time-line, you can adapt this model. It works. And, of course, you will find that this process can have an ending, or it can just go on and on: think, talk, write, read. Thinking, talking, writing, and reading almost always lead to some cognitive good. When you finish, get the kids to *act* on their new ideas. The students in this particular case decided to do oral interviews with various families in the community that would know ways of saying I love you and other customs of particular countries.

As I reflect on this activity, I can see that this group of students learned much about the world and ownership of their own learning. I can see that I learned to trust students' natural curiosity.

Pada, a Hmong American, and Lucille, an African American, recently pointed out to me that this lesson plan is really based on René Descartes's famous first principle: I think; therefore, I am. I continue to learn from my students.

Four Phases #3

Descriptive Phase
Personal Interpretive Phase
Critical Phase
Creative Phase

This model, the Creative Reading Method, was developed by Alma Flor Ada (1988a, 1988b) and is based on the theory and practice of Paulo Freire. She has repeatedly emphasized that the four phases can be interwoven and/or joined in multiple ways.

In the *descriptive phase*, students receive new knowledge from the text, teacher, or technology. Who, where, and when are the questions that focus the initial approach to learning. Typically, this phase of the lesson design is directed at the comprehension questions included in many texts.

Often, the teacher is presenting information in a whole group setting, or the group has read the same material and is discussing the content.

In the *personal interpretive phase,* students are asked to relate the information from the text to their experiences and feelings. It is in this phase that students begin to construct their own knowledge. For example, the teacher could begin the discussion with questions such as: Have you ever felt, heard, seen anything like this? How did it feel? The teacher encourages students to find meaning and connections to the text information based on their own experiences and their own feelings. Validation of feelings improves self-esteem of the learners.

In the *critical phase,* the learners are asked to compare and contrast the knowledge from the text with their own feelings and experiences. Critical analysis is encouraged as students reflect on their generated knowledge: Is this knowledge valid? Valid to whom? Are culture, class, gender, or race factors in this knowledge? Are there alternatives?

In the final *creative phase*, student reflection becomes action; theory becomes practice. The generated knowledge can be lived in the local community, or the ideas can be presented creatively. For example, science lessons become ecology projects. Story ideas can be rewritten from the students' perspective, or content can be codified or dramatized in multiple ways.

Argelia, a bilingual classroom teacher, has been experimenting with Alma Flor Ada's approach to lesson design in her unit on legends and oral history. As with all teachers, Argelia discovered that she needs to adapt the lesson design to fit the needs of her classroom, which is made up of 50 percent Spanish-speakers and 50 percent English-speakers; the goal is bilingualism and biliteracy for all. The specific lesson was based on a story entitled "La mujer que brillaba aún más que el sol," which comes from the oral history tradition of the Zapoteca Indians in Mexico.

Descriptive Phase

Argelia used the preview-review methodology (content is introduced in one language, the ideas are explored in depth in a second language, and content is reviewed in the first language). The preview is comparable to the anticipatory set of the five-step lesson design or the building on prior knowledge, which is part of the Into, Through, and Beyond lesson plan. In this particular lesson, the preview and review were done in English, each for about one-half hour on different days, and the lesson was implemented in Spanish for more than a week. Argelia and her students discussed who the heroine was, what she looked like, what the people of the village were afraid of, and where the heroine went at the end of the story.

Personal Interpretive Phase

This part of the lesson took several days, as the students interviewed their families about traditional stories that are told in Mexico. The students returned to school with written and oral stories to be shared. Eventually, the classroom was rich with language and pictures that were posted on one entire wall.

Critical Phase

Argelia asked her students to relate the content of the story to their own experiences. During this phase of learning, the students discovered some commonalties and differences with their own lived experiences. This discussion eventually focused on the differences in the students' lives and the lives of their parents and grandparents. Argelia charted the similarities and differences as the children generated the language. The students discovered that their lives were indeed very different from those of their parents.

Creative Phase

Argelia's students decided they wanted to divide into groups and act out this story. The families were invited, and each small group shared their creative and rewritten version of the original story.

Just as Argelia is experimenting to transform her personal approach to lesson design, so are her students *transforming* the content of the story into a rewritten play that they are *producing* for their families.

Four Phases #4

> Bringing in the World
> Negotiating the World
> Utilizing the World
> Recreating the World

María is a classroom teacher who continually uses the lens of critical pedagogy to improve the teaching and learning within her classroom. This year she has been reflecting on discipline plans. We designed the following plan to approach discipline under a broader theme of negotiation throughout the curriculum. Originally, we used seven steps; the students soon taught us that four was better for them. The teacher's role is as an investigating partner with the students. The format can be modified or adjusted to fit the context.

María and I wanted to create a lesson format that encourages the development of negotiation, inquiry, and ownership of knowledge by increasing student participation. Our goal was to shift the classroom power from the teacher to the students. We did not want to maintain a structure based on a single source of authority and control; rather, we wanted to encourage social investigation based on collaboration among the students and teacher. The following example took place when the students and María were focusing on negotiation as a form of conflict resolution to be used instead of other discipline models.

Bringing in the World

"What are your experiences with negotiation skills as a form of conflict resolution?" María asked. As they spoke, she recorded their responses on a large piece of paper. María made a particular effort to validate those triggered experiences the students recalled although seemingly unrelated to the topic. If it mattered to the students, it mattered to her. As the students are very interested in mass media, she encouraged references to popular culture. Conflict and negotiation in music, movies, and television were linked to their discussion. After the initial whole group discussion, the students decided to maintain reflective journals with a daily log of conflicts and resolutions. They also agreed to chart their feelings during conflict and resolution.

The students and teacher together created a list of core readings that demonstrated various forms of negotiation skills. María introduced her students to a wide range of material that she previously had placed in the classroom. The students decided they would identify and record negotiation skills implemented by characters as they read their books.

Negotiating the World

"What do you want to know about negotiation skills?" María asked the students the next day in order to encourage their ownership of the learning. The students began to discuss differences in conflict resolution; they noticed different ways of negotiating peaceful resolutions. In small groups, the students continued their own brainstorming, dialogue, and codification. The next day the small groups reported their new discoveries and questions to the class.

Utilizing the World

"Where can you go to find out more about conflict resolution and negotiation skills?" María asked. The students generated a list that included more books, magazines, music, their families, and the social studies book. During the next week the small groups recorded all they had learned from these sources and reported their findings to the class.

Recreating the World

"What can you do now as a result of knowing more about negotiation skills as a form of conflict resolution?" María asked. These students were accustomed to this phase of the lesson format because during this year they have previously turned science into ecological practices at home; math into student budgets; literacy into pen-pal activities. The students knew they would be expected to turn their learning into life. In this case, they decided to use their new knowledge about negotiation skills as a form of conflict resolution playground (Wink & Almanzo, 1995).

Three Phases

Doing critical pedagogy is grounded in some form of Freire's legacy of problem posing.

---

to name

to reflect critically

to act

Stephanie listened as her students discussed their frustration with never being able to open their applesauce containers, which were served at lunch. The students consistently had to ask a teacher or an aide to open the containers for them. Instead of dismissing this topic as irrelevant because it was outside of the prescribed curriculum, Stephanie recognized the dynamic as one that mattered to students. As the students talked, Stephanie wrote their comments on the chalkboard. Stephanie allowed time for the students to articulate and conceptualize the problem. After the students had clearly named their problem, she asked them what could be done to alleviate this problem. The suggestions began as Stephanie continued to capture all the thoughts and language on the chalkboard. Finally, the group came to a consensus. They decided to write a class letter to the company. With the language on the board, the students were able to write independently to express their concerns. When we last called Stephanie, she reported the letters had been mailed, and they were awaiting a reply.

In this case, Stephanie and the students recreated their socially generated knowledge to act upon one small condition of their own world. The transformative lesson design encourages students to act on their knowledge, and it seeks to create processes whereby students can see that their actions do count. Learning and teaching are integrated for self and social transformation.

Two Phases

Dawn and I created this model for her work with adult English-language learners. She was struggling with some of the other models, but found that this worked well for her. She has two goals each week: to bring in *their* world, and to bring in *the* world. During the first phase, *their* world, all language and ideas are codified; stories and narrations, written; and action, planned. The curriculum for the second goal, *the* world, is newspaper, radio, TV, and magazines. The list below includes some of the themes that they generated and explored in class.

Their World
My favorite childhood memory is . . .
The memories I want my children to have are . . .
If I could change the world, I would . . .

The World
Floods, rescues, modes of transportation and communication during storms; (it rained a lot that semester); taxes; immigration; housing; Bosnia, violence; government, and the State of the Union Address. (One of the action plans that followed was a group letter to the president, which received a reply.)

One Phase–No Phase–Mrs. A.

Mrs. A. is a holistic teacher and does not want to hear about steps. You probably couldn't get her to follow a curriculum scope and sequence or a step-by-step recipe. However, she constantly reflects and challenges herself in ways that exceed any prescription.

Democracy with Kids. Mrs. A. teaches in the school where Mark (Democracy with Teachers) is the principal. She was one of the teachers who attended the same labor relations workshop as Mark did. Mrs. A. had long ago implemented what she hoped would be democratic processes in her classroom. However, after the intensive staff development session she critically reflected on the processes and wanted to increase the amount of student participation and responsibilities.

> *I have several morning activities that the students and I always do together; the rule-making process is just one of them. The students participate in a heads-together session before volunteering a rule for the week. Each rule is recorded on the front board. Then I review each rule and ask if there are any objections, questions, or clarifications. Discussion and categorizing occur simultaneously in this process. Every Monday morning, the board is soon filled with many suggestions. However, in order not to overwhelm the students with too many rules, each student votes for four rules from the large list. The four rules with the most votes become the rules for the week. For example, the rules for the first week were:*
>
> *1. No talking when the teacher is talking.*
> *2. No fighting.*
> *3. No running in the classroom.*
> *4. No fighting in the classroom.*
>
> *Since implementing this model of discipline, I have observed that the students are accepting ownership and responsibility for a safer classroom environment.*

This process has led this class to discuss and question the nature of rules and to explore the consequences of their actions. The students are beginning to understand how rules can sometimes benefit some and not others. These are the types of questions that give us and our students reference points for reflecting on democratic processes in our communities, whether they be classrooms for students or meeting rooms for teachers and administrators.

Just as Mrs. A. and her co-workers have become partners in rule making with their administrator, so have her students assumed responsibilities for their individual and group behaviors within the classroom. This critical-social model encourages self-reflected behavior awareness. I know Mrs. A. and Mark and their school fairly well. I am confident that if he had insisted that she and the teachers use one specific discipline plan, she would have resisted. However, Mrs. A. and her students together have created a plan for themselves that they control and that works for them. I think she is doing critical pedagogy (Wink & Almanzo, 1995).

Critical Activities within the Community

Democracy with Families.   In a discussion of family and community involvement with Dawn, she wanted to know "how-to-do-it." I reminded her of the various family and school activities she had experienced with me while she was growing up. It suddenly occurred to us that we were describing two very different approaches to school-sponsored family involvement. One approach is much more democratic. It seems that even when we do not see our beliefs, they continually tend to turn into behaviors that run around behind us and tell stories for all the world to hear. This happens even when we deny our beliefs. I am sure that both sides of the paradigm in Figure 4.2 think they are very democratic. However, the actual implementation of theory to practice tells a very different story.

The following activities are effective in working with families, or they can be used in a classroom. Bonnie and David Freeman have written of various critical approaches to teaching and learning (Freeman & Freeman, 1992). In the first approach, they build on the idea of codification and clarify what it might actually look like in a classroom. I have made small adaptations of their original Questioning Lesson plan.

Questioning Lesson Plan.   The following questions are used to guide the discussion of any theme, in any context, for any group of learners. This model can be used to facilitate a critical and democratic discussion with community groups or with students of all ages. One person can lead the group through small and whole group sharing. It is important for one person to record, on paper or the chalkboard, the participants' words and ideas.

- What is the question worth talking about?
- How does the question fit into the overall plan?
- How will you learn what the students already know?
- What strategies can you use to explore the question?
- What materials will you need?
- What steps will facilitate the learning?
- How will you observe the learning?

Family Graph Activity.   The following activity emerged when the graduate students in a class were creating oral histories. It is designed to demonstrate how much change has taken place in each person's life. It can be

Models for Parental Involvement

The We-Are-Going-To-Do-This-To-You Model of Parental Involvement
or
The We-Are-Going-To-Do-This-With-You Model of Parental Involvement

DOIN' IT TO 'EM	DOIN' IT WITH 'EM
Goal	
change the parents	change the schools
Objectives	
to melt into the pot	to melt the pot
to discuss building community	to build community
Characteristics of the Meetings	
teachers talk	teachers listen
families listen	families talk
families sit still	families interact
everyone leaves immediately after	people hang around
people leave space between them	people hug
kids go to a room with a sitter	kids work with families
teachers tell objectives	families tell stories
Result	
Dysfunctional School	Functional School

FIGURE 4.2 Do it to 'em—Do it with 'em

done in a class in an hour or it can be a month's activities of creating and chronicling a family history and making books. I have found that the participants usually are surprised to learn things about their historical roots that they have never known. All you have to do is to ask the participants to fill in the chart in Figure 4.3 with their own history. After that, just get out of the way. This is student-centered learning.

Star Structure of Success. The following activity is good. Do not be frightened away by the lengthy instructions. It is very simple for one facilitator to organize and will make a lasting impression on the participants. I am indebted to two grad students, LeAnn and Cindy, who created it for one of my classes. I have done it with other groups and have never seen it fail. I am sure the participants have long since forgotten what I said to them, but I am equally sure that they remember what they learned when the ball fell to the floor.

MY FAMILY				
	My Grandparents	My Parents	Me	My Kids
School				
Work Career				
Religion				
Family				
Travel				
Politics				
Beliefs				
Daily Life				

FIGURE 4.3 Family graph

Items Needed for Activity
five participants
large beach ball (the larger the better)
ball of string or long rope
five category cards
picture of star shape

Each participant chooses one of the category cards. The participants form a large circle beginning with one person, who holds the community card. To the right of this person stands the educator, to the right of the educator is the culture and language person, to the right of that person is the administrator. The person representing parents is then placed between the administrator and community. After forming this broad circle with cards in hand, the participants are given these instructions. Facilitator reads:

> *Your first objective is to form the star structure with the ball of rope. You want to build the structure in such a way that the hole in the center of the star has a diameter no greater than eight inches, or about the size of a soccer ball. Please look at the side of your card with the category name, and remember it so that when I call the category you will know to respond.*
>
> *I will begin the action by tossing this ball of rope to the first category that I call. The person with that name on the card is to catch the rope and then read what is printed on side two of the card. When the reading is finished, I will instruct you to hold one end of the rope and toss the remaining ball of rope to the next category called. The next person likewise catches the ball, reads the card, and prepares to hold the rope with one hand while tossing to the next name called.*

Begin the activity by calling out "**community**." The person who has this card catches the ball of rope and reads the card. Call out "**administrator**," and the community representative now holds one end of the rope and tosses the ball of rope to the administrator. The administrator catches the ball of rope and reads the card. Call out "**educator**," and the administrator holds one end of the rope and tosses the ball to the person representing educators. Continue in this way calling "**parents**" next, followed by the person representing "**language and culture**." The person with **language and culture** makes the final toss back to the **community** representative, who holds two ends of the rope together. The formation seen before the group is the large star representing the structure upholding the child, soon to enter the picture. Instruct the participants further. Facilitator reads:

> *Hold tight to your ropes and keep the line taut unless instructed to let it go. You must position yourselves so that the hole in the center can balance the beach ball.*

Place a giant beach ball, which represents a student, in the center of the structure and continue reading. Facilitator continues:

> *The beach ball symbolizes a student in the center of a well-balanced and unified school community in which the student can mature and thrive. All groups are working together for the benefit of that student.*

*Suppose that this student is not thriving in our system, but is falling behind academically. Rather than blaming the student, let us look closer at our structure to find the cause of academic slippage. If the culture and language of that student is not valued in the community and the student is met with disdain for his or her identity, then we have a weakness developing in our structure. **Community** participant, allow the rope to go slack.*

*If the administrators hold a philosophical stance that does not value the student's language and culture, then chances are the educational system will lack effective practices. At this point we find another weakness in the **administrator** side and the **language and culture** side. These participants allow the rope to go slack.*

*Suppose that both the community and the administrators are strong (they tighten rope), but the teachers and parents believe that their students must be mainstreamed as quickly as possible in order to learn English (rope goes slack). We now have weak points in the structure on the **educators**, **parents**, and **language** sides. Moving students away from their heritage language into English as quickly as possible may appear to be logical to those who are not aware of language acquisition principles.*

At any point, you can see that it is easy to drop the ball if these five groups do not work together to support students.

The entire community needs to pull together to assure that the pedagogical processes are beneficial, and not detrimental.

When the ball falls from the center of the star, it is a graphic reminder that students need all of us to work together in order to succeed. Usually participants have lots to say after the ball falls. Now the participants can return to their seats. The activity ends with a discussion of the following ways of teaching and learning.

BENEFICIAL	or	DETRIMENTAL
Cultural Validation	or	Cultural Assimilation
Transformative Class	or	Passive Class
Teacher/Learner	or	Teacher/Transmitter
Questioning	or	Memorizing
Parents/Participants	or	Parents/Spectators

The following are the category cards that the participants read as they form their star. Use index cards with large printing.

COMMUNITY — Sets the philosophy of the school district by mandating to the district school board policies and procedures under which the schools will operate. Communities must rethink traditional values and update attitudes to include the vast multicultural populations that are now a part of our nation.

ADMINISTRATORS carry out the will of the community by enforcing policies established by the school board. Clear philosophical guidelines must be handed down throughout the district. Administrators must keep in touch with the reality of today's classroom and support current research and development.

EDUCATORS research and implement theories and models that support academic growth and development. Teachers must be confident of their professional knowledge about student welfare with regard to academic and social success. They must strive toward meeting individualized needs of their students.

PARENTS — Parental support is vital to academic and social success of children. Parents, as first teachers, must realize the important role they play in the educational future of their children. When working with parents we must consider how we invite them to participate in the education of their children. We must emphasize the importance of their formal and informal teaching skills, and allow them opportunities to provide input into the future academic success of their children.

LANGUAGE AND CULTURE are an important focus in development of positive psychosocial and academic growth. Heritage culture must be targeted and valued for both parent and child. Language and culture must be more than isolated celebrations within the school environment. Students and parents must be made aware of the importance of primary language and academic success. When possible, students must be allowed to build on previously acquired knowledge through their primary language and develop it further.

To do critical pedagogy in the classroom, we must first stop and critically reflect upon the educational processes that we are living and perpetuating daily. We must stop and take time to reflect with our students in our classes. We must stop and listen to what students are saying. The following is a summary of some of the things that might prove advantageous for you. We suspect that none of the following will work unless they are grounded in a community of respect and safety.

Two Ways of Believing and Behaving

Of course, there aren't just two ways—there are multiple ways. However, the following two columns are stereotypical experiences that we've
all had with schools and communities. If the teacher has a transmission
philosophy, the classroom practice might look like the column on the right.
However, if the teacher had a more generative and transformational approach, the activity in the classroom might look more like the column on
the left. It is often helpful to take time to reflect on our own theory and see
how it turns into practice in our daily lives. If you are a teacher and haven't
thought about this for awhile, just ask your students. They will know your
theory because they are living your practice every day—even if you are un-
aware of it. Our theory informs our practice; our beliefs affect our behaviors
in classes.

Theory	
Transformational Philosophy	Transmission Philosophy
Practice	
Students and teacher own knowledge.	Teacher owns the knowledge.
Everyone knows something.	Students get knowledge from teacher.
Start with students.	Start with text.
Purpose: students learn to learn.	Purpose: students learn to memorize.
Lifelong learning has value.	Formal schooling has value.
Community controls schools.	Schools control education.

These two columns have been effective in getting teachers and learners
to understand their own perspective. Often teachers are so busy doing and

meeting deadlines, they don't take time to think about what they actually believe today and how they might turn those beliefs into behaviors in the classroom.

A MESS

I have saved the best activity for last. I encourage you to adapt this and try it. Make it work for you. There are surprises every time you enter into this type of process.

First, you start with a mess. In this case, a mess is any situation within an educational space that needs attention. It is something that is not working for someone; it is the *phony*. I probably should change the name to: Find the Phony.

I adapted this framework from Lieberman (1986) and García (1993). Tove Skutnabb-Kangas also has influenced this model; she immediately thought of the mess as creative chaos. I have been experimenting with various groups with this particular process, and so far, it is has been extremely powerful for all involved. In each case, we needed a minimum of three hours walking though the process. We worked in small groups at each phase and shared with the whole group after each phase. The commitment statement (the last step, which is really the first) is fundamental to the cyclical process. When you finish, each participant will have made a commitment to change, and each participant will leave with new questions. In all fairness, I must mention that this process does not lead to smaller messes; it leads to more critical questions.

Before beginning the steps of this process, the facilitator and the participants need to generate a list of messes. What are the problems? concerns? questions? The facilitator captures all the ideas and records for all to see. The facilitator begins by asking each member of the whole group to reflect privately before joining a smaller group. After this, the facilitator again records more questions from the group. Next, the participants are encouraged to sit in small groups by messes. Those who are interested in a particular question can problem pose as a small group. Once in the small group, the facilitator asks that each member individually shares her concern with the small group. Once this has happened, each small group is given the following format to guide their discussion.

First, You Start with a Mess

Start with a mess (problem, contradiction, difficult situation).
Define it. Name it.

Learn more about it.
How can we learn more about this?
Who knows what about this?
How will we share information with the group?

Alternative approaches.
List all of the ideas that might work. Think wildly and passionately.
Dream. Think up utopias.
Collectively, choose an approach.

Preparation.
What are the roadblocks? How can we prepare for them?
What new problems might this approach create? What are possible solutions for these new problems? What could go wrong? What role might others play if we decide to try to change this?

Action plan and evaluation.
Create a timeline and plan of action.
Do it; fix it. Do it; fix it.

Write a commitment statement.
We commit to . . .
I commit to . . .
Members of the group share personal commitment statements and agree to use their own expertise to help fix the mess.

Begin again.
Redefine and rename the new mess.

At times, I have streamlined the process into the following steps. Depending on the participants and the amount of time available to you, try it in the following manner.

Find a mess.

Learn more about it.

What could be some alternative approaches?

Action plan and evaluation.

Write a commitment statement.

Name a new mess.

This is not a one-shot activity; rather, it is the beginning of more critical teaching and learning with colleagues. The commitment statements that end the activity provide authentic experiences in which teachers and learners discover their own power.

What works? We all want to know. I am sure that the answers will vary for each of us. I have tried to summarize what has worked for me in my experiences in schools.

What Works

taking time

tossing the texts

asking: but why?

reflecting

conceptualizing and articulating our own philosophical assumptions

understanding why and how beliefs change

naming the power structures: critically reflecting and acting on them

relearning and unlearning

acknowledging the powerful emotions of power, racism, classism, sexism

understanding and being able to articulate the new global realities

challenging our long-held assumptions about teaching and learning

reading hard books

entering into dialogue

recognizing the contradictions in our own lives

recognizing our own power, expertise, knowledge, and role

seeing with new eyes

taking time and creating a safe place!

Recently, a teacher suddenly raised his hand and told me that you can't really *do* critical pedagogy; it is more a state of mind. I agree. It calls on us to see and to know in new critical ways. It calls upon us to reexamine our own assumptions. We don't *do* critical pedagogy; we *live* it. We are challenged to live our beliefs. Each of us has a set of beliefs about values and education. These beliefs come to life everyday in our behaviors in the classroom. What is it that each of us believes? Why do we believe this? Have our beliefs changed? An examination of our own beliefs and accompanying behaviors can lead each of us to rethink our approach to teaching and learning in our own classrooms.

"If you watch a teacher long enough, you will know her beliefs. I call this the Belief Indicator," Gary said to his classmates in the teaching credential program.

"The what?" his classmates said in unison.

"The Belief Indicator," he said. "Just watch your professors; they all have one. What they do every day in class tells you all about their beliefs. It always reminds me of the old adage: The eyes are the window to the soul. I think the methods are the windows to a teacher's philosophy."

Obviously, Gary understands my thesis. Just as Gary told his classmates, our behaviors are a reflection of our beliefs; our practice reflects our theory.

The purpose of transformative education is to create processes whereby students can see that their actions do count. They are encouraged to take the learning from the classroom and to engage locally and socially. This model of learning and teaching assumes that the generation of knowledge in the classroom leads to the betterment of life for the student or for the community. Knowledge is created to influence their world; it is no longer a passive ingredient designed only for the classroom. Research supports teachers, such as Stephanie, capturing small moments of truth to create curriculum that directly relates to a felt need of the class (Caine & Caine, 1991).

I ask one central question: Why do we do what we do? In the spirit of reflective teaching and learning, in the spirit of attempting to learn *how* to do critical pedagogy, I challenge you, the readers, to reflect critically on your own philosophy and how it is reflected in your practice. There is no one best way to *do* critical pedagogy, but all ways involve critical reflection by teachers and learners together.

LOOKING AHEAD FOR ELUSIVE METHODS

How do you think you *do* critical pedagogy?

NOTE

1. Others have used different language to describe these three approaches to lesson design. Of course, there really are more than these three approaches; it is a continuum of teacher-controlled learning to student-centered learning; from transmission to transformation. For further reading, I encourage you to see Freeman and Freeman (1994) *Between worlds: Access to second language acquisition*, published by Heinemann of Portsmouth, NH. In this book, they adapt the language of Lindfors (1982) and describe these three approaches as student as plant, builder, and explorer. The student as plant relates to the transmission model of education in that the teacher provides the students with all that the student needs. The idea of the student as builder reflects the constructive and generative approaches to knowledge and literacy. The student as explorer moves on the continuum towards transformational teaching and learning. *Rethinking Schools* (1995) also explores these various approaches to teaching and learning (see note 1, chapter 3).

chapter 5

Critical Pedagogy
Why in the World Does It Matter?

Kids matter. That's why. Our future matters. That's why. It is as simple as that. It also is something we all know. This is serious business we are talking about. Students and teachers are hurting. We in education are a mirror of society that is more and more polarized.

But, are poles really so bad? Let's relook and rethink poles. Aren't poles just opposite ways of thinking? Yes. Is diversity of thought bad? No. Would it really be so good if we all thought alike? I doubt it. Aren't poles just an example of multiple voices and multiple ways of knowing? I think so. Are schools big enough for diversity? It's who we are.

We come from a tradition that assumed that *differences* were bad. Critical pedagogy teaches us to look again and to see again and to know in new ways that are a true reflection of today. Diversity of thought is good for schools and good for society.

Throughout this book, I have tried to show the many contradictions and changes we all are experiencing in our educational spaces. These contradictions and changes often frighten and offend us at first; they feel like polar opposites. We resist, we deny, we object. Critical pedagogy has helped me welcome these contradictions and changes. The poles no longer tear me apart. The poles are just a part of a larger picture that is our ever-increasing vibrant society.

The world is changing fast, and these societal changes are reflected every day in our schools. Every newspaper we pick up tells us again and again that what we are doing is not working. Historically, our schools are based on the needs of an agrarian society in which knowledge was controlled and transmitted by the schools. At the rate with which new knowledge and information is now being generated, it is impossible for even the very best teacher to be able to transmit it all. Students of the future need to be able to access new knowledge, critically reflect upon it, interpret it, and apply it in new ways. The changing world is dragging us (kicking and screaming, in some instances) into the world of a transformative model of education. The purpose of education is to transform society into a truly democratic environment for all.

James Cummins has spoken repeatedly about the changing global realities, which he calls cultural, linguistic, scientific, technological, and ecological realities. In the new global realities, diversity of people and diversity of thought is the norm. This is the foundation for a thriving society; it is only when change ceases that societies begin to die. In a vibrant, dynamic society diversity of thought enriches us all. More recently, this idea of global realities (Cummins & Sayers, 1995) has been expanded and now includes the idea of "existential realities," which encompasses the sense of fragility we experience in our relationship with the physical and social environment.

Cummins's idea of the new global realities certainly is affirmed in my own experiences. I rarely visit a school that is not multicultural, and many are multilingual. It appears to me that the mainstream is very multicultural. These changing global realities lead us to ask ourselves: What do students today need to know in order to thrive and flourish in the future? What are the needs of students and citizens of the twenty-first century?

STUDENTS OF THE TWENTY-FIRST CENTURY

We will need bilingual/biliterate students who love to read, can reflect critically, and live their lives with passion and action. We need collaborative, lifelong learners who are responsible for their own learning and understand that it comes from their lived experiences. We need students who can generate new knowledge and apply it in unknown ways. We need students who can write and rewrite their world from a pluralistic perspective, students who can pose problems and solve problems with technology that stretches beyond our wildest thoughts. We need students who know how to access, interpret, and critically use new and emerging information. Above all, our students will need to be able to work in a multilingual and multicultural society. The students who will thrive socially and economically are those who bravely cross borders: cultural, linguistic, classist, sexist, and racial. We must begin with every teacher and every student and family in every school today. As a local teacher/graduate student wrote at the end of an essay: *My goal is to begin today*. I think that teacher has something to teach all of us.

I recently asked a group of teachers how they thought we should teach critically and effectively for the students of the twenty-first century. Their answers are worth sharing.

How to Teach for Students of the Twenty-First Century

Be passionate about your subject matter.

Know students and their backgrounds.

Involve the families as citizens of the classroom.

Allow students the freedom to explore and time to sit and think.

Provide meaningful, practical, and relevant information.

Show students how to access and generate new information.

Ask "why" a lot.

Make sure students see you reading.

The writing of this book has pushed me along my own unlearning curve. If anyone had told me five years ago that my study of critical pedagogy would bring me to this point, I never would have believed it. Even a year ago, I would not have believed it. However, by writing my own thoughts, I have discovered some of my own elusive answers. First, I seek my answers in the delicate balance between a caring heart and a critical eye. Second, I follow the path of action that is in that enlightened and precarious place between courage and patience. And, third, this all takes time.

THE PEDAGOGY OF A CARING HEART AND CRITICAL EYES

It might seem at first that *caring* is poles apart from *critical*. Not for me. They are two parts of a new dynamic pedagogical whole. For me, the critical perspective and the centrality of caring come together under the framework of critical pedagogy. And no one is more surprised than I. I find strength in these seeming opposites. They fit in a new whole picture of schools. A complex picture. A diverse picture. A vibrant picture. And, a very exciting and powerful new picture of the potential within all of us. Critical pedagogy has painted this new picture for me.

A Caring Heart

Why should kids care, if we don't? Caring counts. I would like to see teachers and learners enter into dialogue of some very fundamental human needs that are not being met in our schools. For example, love. It's true, love trumps methods! I really have felt this for a long time, but I had to be patient until I had enough courage to say it. Critical pedagogy brought me here. I believe this is what McLaren is alluding to when he speaks of the *teachable heart*.

I suggest that all of us in education should place our entire discussion of teaching and learning into a larger framework of caring. Nel Noddings has been a consistent voice in raising questions of ethics and values in schools. National educational journals are alive with the importance of caring. But, a national teacher of the year said it best when referring to a former teacher who had turned his life around: "He put his hands on my shoulder that first day of class and it burned clear through to my heart" (Hanson, 1994, pp. A1, A11). As we live through these rapid social and demographic changes, I suspect that caring counts. Nowhere are these changes experienced more profoundly than in schools everyday.

We come from varying perspectives, experiences, academic areas, but we all care about teaching and learning. In a safer world, that would be enough. However, in the social-cultural context of education of the 1990s, it is not enough. We also must care about ourselves, our colleagues, our students, and our communities. As Elam (1995) comments:

> In a more reasonable society, in a more perfect nation, in a world beyond ugly discriminations of gender, race, and class, our citizens would live in a convivial atmosphere of community. . . . That is why I worry a good deal about the soundness of the national mind and spirit. I worry about public voices that tout intolerance and narrow-mindedness. I worry about the politics of parsimony and isolation. . . . I still take comfort knowing that singular acts of care and compassion take place all the time and I hope for the day when these acts will become the very core of our culture. (p. A11)

Pedagogical caring must be balanced within the dialectic of a critical stance to meet the needs of teaching and learning for the twenty-first century. Critically reflecting on theory and practice, and acting on our individual praxis, is fundamental to critical pedagogy. A caring heart can be demonstrated in innumerable ways in the classroom and community. But, a critically caring heart moves us along a critical path of unlearning.

The caring heart does not mean that we stop listening to the whispering of the juxtaposition: the critically reflective eye. Do not be fooled. Caring teachers and learners continue to look in the mirror, the classroom, and the community to discover their own path of unlearning. The caring heart and the critical eye often bring us to that enlightened and contradictory place where each begins to detect elusive answers.

A Critical Eye

Why should kids critically reflect, if we don't? Teachers often talk about the importance of inquiry; of critical reflection; of active and engaged investigation. But, if we don't, they won't.

The end of this century will force us to know in new ways, as Carole, a high school teacher, discovered:

> *A very profound learning experience shaped me as a teacher. When I first began my career, I had high "standards" for my students. It was to the point of being uncaring. After two years, I decided that love and compassion were more important than strict regulations. Today, the students and their outlook on life are more important than a rule. The irony is that as I begin to focus more on caring about the whole student and less about "standards" and "regulations," the students are learning more. I thought I was exchanging high "standards" for a little caring. The truth is the opposite: As I care more, the students learn more.*

Carole's experiences demonstrate just how confounding contradictions can be. Carole thought she used to have *high standards*. But, since she began to critically reflect on her own practice, she has discovered that the students have higher standards for their own learning.

In the preface, I mentioned a friend who had told me 30 years ago that teachers can hurt kids. I told you I was shocked and did not (want to) believe it. Kim is a teacher who critically reflects on her own theory and practice. She challenges herself to look again and see again. But, even I was surprised when I read her paper, which crossed my desk. In this story she brings together the importance of a critical perspective, which can often lead us to a caring philosophical stance.

> *My first-grade teacher was a monster.* (Kim wrote this with a black felt tipped pen, underlined the work, <u>monster</u>.) *She was mean. She liked to yell and threaten.*
>
> *One day someone turned out the lights while we were walking back to class from music. When we got back to class, she asked, "Who turned off the lights?" I remember how frightened and quiet we were.*
>
> *"Nobody is leaving this room today until the person that did this confesses," she yelled at us. The bell rang to go home and still no one confessed. We sat. We sat for what seemed to be a long time.*

"I did it," I finally said. I was scared because I didn't think the teacher was going to let us go home. The other students were dismissed, and I had to stay in the room alone with the teacher. I remember her cold voice asking me why I had done it.

"I didn't. I just said it so we could go home," I said as I started to cry.

She called me a liar. I remember the shame I felt. I will never forget that day.

My critical reflections of this experience have made me believe in the importance of caring in the classroom.

PEDAGOGY OF COURAGE AND PATIENCE

I also have started to notice that my years with students and my reading of all those critical theory books have led me to focus more and more on courage and patience. Once again, you may sense that courage and patience are poles apart. Not for me. They are part of that new pedagogical whole. Courage, sometimes. Patience other times. Only reflective action will help you decide which one when.

Just as teaching and learning is a dialectical union that propels our professional growth forward, so is the union of courage and patience fundamental to our pedagogy for the future. Daily, I feel the pull of courage and the counterpull of patience. Often times we need to be as courageous as the context will allow. Other times patience is our greatest ally: patience with ourselves, our colleagues, our context.

Presently, I am watching a district completely divided into two camps. I will call the two teams the White Sox and the Brown Sox. The school is divided, the community is divided, and all are being hurt. In the middle of this great battle is a young, beginning teacher, an ethnic minority who is being pummeled by the White Sox team. It appears to me that when the dust settles, the Board of Education will offer a contract for another year to the young teacher — a move that will outrage the White Sox and please the Brown Sox. I predict the young teacher will keep his job unless he leaves in complete discouragement, which probably is the hidden objective of the White Sox players. I watch the young teacher struggle to be courageous and defend himself; I watch him be patient with his adversaries. I can see the principal is walking a tight rope in her balance between courage and patience. They are in good company: "Paulo Freire lived the dialectic between patience and impatience. He had to be patient, impatiently. It was necessary to be impatient, patiently" (Gadotti, 1994, p. 47).

Candi is a teacher/grad student who works in a very coercive school setting. She understands that the school believes in transmission model education. Candi sees herself as a transformative educator. She has critically reflected and understands the barriers she faces. Candi also knows that her life is in this community, and she must find ways of living, learning, and teaching. She asked if we could use a class session to problem pose on her struggles with her environment. She shared honestly, as did her colleagues in the graduate class. At the end of this challenging session, they generated a plan based on the dialectical union of courage and patience. They decided Candi would commit to:

1. be courageous enough to live her beliefs honestly;
2. be courageous enough to invite her coteachers and administrators to her room when she would be *doing* a lesson design based on critical pedagogy;
3. be patient enough to let her colleagues draw their own conclusions;
4. be patient enough to listen and be courageous enough to repeat back adversarial comments;
5. be courageous enough to accept the fact that she can't control others' beliefs; she can only live her own.

One year later Candi reports that her acceptance of the dialectical union of courage and patience has lead her to be a more joyful and rigorous teacher. And, she likes her colleagues and school better. Candi recognizes that she herself must be courageous and patient before she asks it of her students.

TIME.   TIME.   TIME.

All of this takes time. For example, the language of critical pedagogy takes time. The thoughts of critical pedagogy take time. Jonathan's literacy took time. A *teachable heart* takes time. Critically reflective practice takes time. Challenging our own intellect takes time. Reading books on critical pedagogy takes time. Shifting our lesson designs takes time. Shifting our paradigm *really* takes time.

Time is more important than *coverage*. The elusive answers that are meaningful for me all seem to be grounded in issues of time. Traditionally, we have been driven by the pedagogy of *coverage*. We have to *cover* this, now. We have to *cover* that, next. However, *coverage* is not as important as learning. What good does it do to cover the material in the time allowed if students don't know it? As Jonathan said, "Even if I know how to spell *aboard* on Friday, I won't know it next Monday." Time traditionally controls teachers; I suggest that it ought to be the other way around. I also think that we, as educators, must continually reflect on coverage and time.

Why should we expect kids to take time, if we don't? Recently, a former master's graduate called to tell me about a statistics class in her doctoral program. The professor, who was very intimidating, came to every class with 50 problems to cover. The frightened and frustrated students were not learning, but he continued to cover his 50 stat problems. The students endured for several class periods. They sat quietly and passively and copied every number and every squiggle that he wrote on the board. But, in all of this time, no one was *learning*, they were only *covering* his prescribed curriculum, 50 problems per class. The students were still too nervous to question him. Finally, in desperation, this former master's student raised her hand to ask for help in class.

STUDENT: Professor, I did not understand the first problem. Would you please repeat your explanation?

PROFESSOR: No, I have no time to repeat; I have 49 more problems to cover.

STUDENT: Yes, but if I don't understand number one, it really doesn't matter what you do with the remaining 49.

This particular example screams of the dangers of the pedagogy of coverage. This professor thought he needed to *cover* 50 problems in the allotted time. Students don't need to *cover* 50 problems; they need to learn. We, as educators, need to reflect on our perspective of time. We feel controlled by time. However, in our own classes, we need to control the time.

The student had been patient, and now was moving to courage. If only the professor had been courageous enough to be patient with his students' learning.

Jonathan's teacher felt that he had to *cover* spelling words every Monday; he felt that he had to test every Friday. But Jonathan realized that the students needed to *know* the words — even on the next Monday.

I struggle with coverage and time in every class. I come in with my objectives, my gorgeous transparencies, my planned organization of the three-hour block of time. The students keep interrupting me with meaningful questions. They keep relating their new knowledge from class to their own world. That darned transformative learning! It has even driven me to say, "Stop this learning, I want to teach!"

TEACHERS TAUGHT ME, TOO

Throughout this book, I have written about the many things students taught me to learn and unlearn:

- teaching is learning;
- if it doesn't matter to students, it doesn't matter;
- change and contradictions are in every classroom.

In this chapter, I have told you how critical pedagogy comes together for me in new and surprising ways. Critical pedagogy has helped me understand that it is okay to be critical of processes that we don't philosophically support; it is okay to care a lot. Critical pedagogy has given me courage and taught me lessons of patience. And, it is okay if all of this takes time.

Thirty years ago when I started teaching, no one could have told me that teaching would bring me to this way of knowing. Education classes didn't teach me these important lessons; students did. We need to listen to and learn more from students. With changes happening so fast in our society today, I cannot imagine what students will teach me in the next 10 years. However, I am anxious to learn whatever it will be.

Now, a final word about teachers. The truth is that I have been blessed with the best, and I have learned from them.

What Teachers Taught Me

Caring counts.
Mem Fox

Learning should be rigorous and joyful.
Paulo Freire

Teachers are intellectuals.
Henry Giroux

Coercive relations of power don't work; collaborative relations do.
James Cummins

Meaning matters.
Stephen Krashen

Good teachers and learners start with a teachable heart.
Peter McLaren

A Teams and B Teams are good for the A Team.
Tove Skutnabb-Kangas

It's fun to talk with a friend while we learn.
Lev Vygotsky

It's okay to learn while we teach.
The Benson Kids

NOW, HERE IS THE POINT

Critical pedagogy is about hope! We all want it. Critical pedagogy led me to it. I started years ago reading those difficult, theoretical books. They made sense to me. I will never forget the first time I read McLaren (1989); I remember thinking: Yes. Yes. Yes. The first time I read Giroux (1988), I remember thinking: This room is vibrating. These books were like the kids I had been teaching. They were not theoretical pages. They were faces and hearts.

When I first began my study of critical pedagogy, I feared I would see too much, too critically. I feared I would lose me in those infuriating new words and old thoughts. However, the opposite has happened again. I'm not so sure these poles are all bad. Confounding contradictions. Critical pedagogy has given me hope.

Why does critical pedagogy matter? It matters because J.J. matters.

> *Steve, a friend who is actively involved within his community, told me this story about a young African American teenage boy, J.J. Steve has a special interest in teenage boys who are lost and adrift. J.J. is almost a stereotype of a marginalized and angry young black man. He comes from an economically disadvantaged family; his father abandoned them many years ago. J.J.'s mom is working hard, for long hours, with low pay. Gangs, drugs, and fast money were becoming more and more appealing to J.J.*
>
> *On this particular occasion, J.J. was in trouble (again) at school, and Steve was called in to talk to him. Steve did not talk. He listened.*
>
> *"You know what you got, and I ain't got? Hope. You got it. I want it," J.J. yelled at Steve.*

Steve and J.J. come from worlds that are poles apart. They are breaking those traditional barriers of race and class. They come together in a safe and social environment (the park) every week. This does not cost anyone anything. Steve and J.J. have committed their time, their courage, and their patience. They care about each other. They critically reflect on ways of generating hope in J.J.'s life. Their story is a powerful mandate for what each of us can do. Must do. The kids and the future matter. "And it is through changing the present that we make the future" (Freire as cited in Gadotti, 1994, p. 148).

TO MAKE A DIFFERENCE

One of the most important lessons that I have ever learned from educators is always to leave them with one final method: something that they can do tomorrow in their own schools and communities. This, then, is my last activity.

Critical pedagogy has been assigned many esoteric and abstract meanings, most of which have enriched my life as a teacher and a learner. This critical perspective will continue to drive my own relearning and unlearning.

Most of us went into education "to make a difference." For many, this phase soon became just another reason to be cynical. Critical pedagogy has not only taken this cynicism away from me, it has given me hope. It has led me to believe that I really can make a difference. Conscientization. Self and social transformation. Empowerment. Problem posing. Praxis. Action. They are no longer words to learn; they are no longer things I *do*; now, they are ideas I strive to *live* every day.

Recently, I have been hearing a story about a particular teacher. In fact, I have heard four different versions of the same story. I will tell the story the way I heard it the first time, although I have since discovered what I assume to be the source of the original story (Bridges, 1993). It seems this teacher decided she would make one small change in her teaching. It would not cost anything. She would not have to ask permission from an administrator. It would not take much of her time. She would not have to go to meetings at night, write a document, and seek the school board's permission. It was just one small change. Maybe, just maybe, she could make a difference.

> *She went to a local trophy shop and ordered blue ribbons that said:* I Make a Difference. *When the ribbons arrived, she reflected seriously on each of her 30 students. Each student was special and had made unique contributions to the class and to her life. She knew she had learned from every one. Reflection. But, she had never taken the time to tell the students. Action. She decided to tell the students in front of the class what she felt was their unique contribution to the class and how each had enriched her life.*
>
> *On the Blue Ribbon Day, she took her time as she expressed her appreciation for each student's distinctive gift to the class and to her life. The students were silent as she spoke and as she pinned a blue ribbon on each shirt right above the heart. She was astounded at the reaction of her students. Some of them had never heard such sincere and honest praise. Many tears and shy smiles expressed their feelings. After the blue ribbon ceremony, she told the class that each of them had to leave with two more ribbons so they, too, could express their appreciation to someone in their life.*
>
> *Eventually, one of these blue ribbons made its way to a young junior executive, Bob, at a large company. He agonized what he should do with his. He was the supervisor for many employees. He went through each name and finally decided he had to give the blue ribbon to his boss, Paul Long, who had a reputation for being*

unapproachable, elitist, and grumpy. Everyone, including the junior executives, avoided him.

With butterflies in his stomach, he knocked on the office door of the CEO.

"Come in," Mr. Long grumbled. It was clear to Bob that his boss was distracted, busy, and did not want to be disturbed.

"Mr. Long, I am here to tell you that I appreciate you as the visionary leader of this company. Without your forethought and planning, we would never be able to succeed in this business. You make a difference in my life, and you make a valuable contribution in this community. I would like permission to reach across your desk and pin a blue ribbon on your shirt." Bob pinned the I Make a Difference *blue ribbon on the pocket of his CEO.*

Paul was speechless. He finally managed to mumble his appreciation. Bob left the office with a sense that he had chosen the right person.

"Mr. Long, here is another blue ribbon. You need to pin it on someone who has made a difference in your life," Bob said as he placed a second blue ribbon on Paul's large desk.

Paul Long went home to his family. He did not mention what had happened at work that day. His family did not notice his silence because it was his custom to eat dinner and then to talk on the phone in his den. However, tonight Paul was thinking about who should receive his blue ribbon. He finally decided.

He walked down the hallway to the his son's bedroom. His son, Paul, Jr., was seventeen years old.

"Son, I know that I often don't speak honestly with you. I know that I am often too busy. But, I want you to know that you make all the difference in my life." As he said this, Paul, Sr. reached over and pinned the I Make a Difference *blue ribbon on Paul, Jr.*

His son began to cry and was soon sobbing. His head hung and his shoulders were heaving up and down with each sob.

"Son, what is the matter?" his dad said.

"Dad, no one ever told me that I make a difference. I had been planning on committing suicide tomorrow, and now I don't have to do it."

What good is this story if we don't turn it into action? Critical pedagogy has taught me that my actions can make a difference. Beginning this semester, I will award an *I Make a Difference* blue ribbon to each of my grad students/teachers. I will make time to tell my students how they make a difference in the community of our classroom and in my life. And, I will give each of them more blue ribbons that they can pass on to their students or others in their life. Dawn will be doing the same thing with her new group of fourth graders.

Won't you join us? I will begin to collect all the stories that demonstrate how each of us can make a difference. Without studying critical pedagogy for years, I would never have had the courage to do this, nor the patience to wait for the stories of power, love, and caring.

LOOKING AHEAD FOR MORE ELUSIVE ANSWERS

"Life," said Izzy, "is a series of strange and seemingly pointless stories. Meaning is derived from a relationship of story, storyteller, and listener. By far the hardest task is that of the listener."

(Kaminsky, 1991, p. 84, as cited in Vallance, 1995)

You are the listener. Why in the world does critical pedagogy matter to you? This book is filled with my stories, my ideas, my perspective, my experiences, my biases, my voice. However, I think this book would be more valuable if you would read and write *with* me. Reading is one way of acquiring knowledge. Writing is one way of inquiring into your own knowledge. Write your stories, your ideas, your perspective, your experiences, your biases, your voice, and your ways of knowing. Critical pedagogy has taught me to be a listener and a storyteller. I encourage you to listen and tell your stories.

How should I end this book? Of course, with a beginning: Yours! Why should we expect kids to write, if we don't?

Bibliography

Ada, A. F. (1988a). Creative reading: A relevant methodology for language minority children. In L. M. Malave (Ed.), *NABE '87. Theory, research and application: Selected papers* (pp. 97–111). Buffalo: State University of New York Press.

Ada, A. F. (1988b). The Pájaro Valley experience: Working with Spanish-speaking parents to develop children's reading and writing skills in the home through the use of children's literature. In T. Skutnabb-Kangas & J. Cummins (Eds.), *Minority education: From shame to struggle* (pp. 223–238). Philadelphia, PA: Multilingual Matters.

Bancroft, A. (1995, March 28). 20 Years of affirmative action: Still no parity. *The Modesto Bee*, p. A8.

Blanck, G. (1990). Vygotsky: The man and his cause. In L. Moll (Ed.), *Vygotsky and education* (pp. 31–58). New York: Cambridge University Press.

Bowles, S., & Gintis, H. (1976). *Schooling in capitalist America*. New York: Basic Books.

Bridges, H., (1993). Who you are makes a difference. In J. Canfield & M. V. Hanson (Eds.), *Chicken soup for the soul* (pp.19–21). Deerfield Beach, FL: Health Communications.

Caine, R., & Caine, G. (1991). *Making connections: Teaching and the human brain*. Alexandria, VA: Association for Supervision and Curriculum Development.

Canfield, J., & Hanson, M. V. (Eds.) (1993). *Chicken soup for the soul*. Deerfield Beach, FL: Health Communications.

Carnes, J. (1995, Spring). Home was a horse stall. *Teaching Tolerance*, 50–57.

Cortés, C. (Ed.). (1986). *The education of language minority students: A contextual interaction model.* Los Angeles: Evaluation, Dissemination, and Assessment Center, California State University.

Cremin, L. (1964). *The transformation of the school.* New York: Vantage Books.

Cummins, J. (1989). *Empowering minority students.* Sacramento: California Association for Bilingual Education.

Cummins, J. (1994). The socioacademic achievement model in the context of coercive and collaborative relations of power. In R. DeVillar, C. Faltis, & J. Cummins (Eds.), *Cultural diversity in schools: From rhetoric to practice* (pp. 363–390). Albany: State University of New York Press.

Cummins, J., & Sayers, D. (1995). *Brave new schools: Challenging cultural illiteracy.* New York: St. Martin's Press.

Edelsky, C. (1991). *With literacy and justice for all: Rethinking the social in language and education.* Bristol, PA: Falmer Press.

Elam, R. (1995, March 3). Voices of reason and compassion. *The Modesto Bee*, p. A11.

Fader, D. N., & McNeil, E. B. (1966). *Hooked on books: Program & proof.* New York: Berkley Medallion Books.

Faltis, C. (1990). Freirian and Vygotskian perspective. *Foreign Language Annals, 23*(2), 117–126.

Fox, M. (1993). *Radical reflections: Passionate opinions on teaching, learning, and living.* San Diego, CA: Hartcourt Brace & Company.

Freeman, Y., & Freeman, D. (1992). *Whole language for second language learners.* Portsmouth, NH: Heinemann.

Freeman, Y., & Freeman, D. (1994). *Between worlds: Access to second language acquisition.* Portsmouth, NH: Heinemann.

Freire, P. (1974). *Pedagogy of the oppressed.* New York: Seabury Press.

Freire, P. (1993, February 4). *Teaching and learning.* Paper presented at the California Association for Bilingual Education, Anaheim, CA.

Freire, P. (1994). *The pedagogy of hope: Reliving pedagogy of the oppressed.* New York: Continuum Publishing Group.

Freire, P., & Macedo, D. (1987). *Literacy: Reading the word and the world.* South Hadley, MA: Bergin & Garvey.

Gadotti, M. (1994). *Reading Paulo Freire: His Life and Work.* Albany: State University of New York Press.

García, H. S. (1993). Shifting the paradigms of education and language policy: Implications for language minority children. *The Journal of Educational Issues of Language Minority Students* (12), 1–6.

Gee, J. (1990). *Social linguistics andl iteracies: Ideology in discourses.* Bristol, PA: Falmer Press.

Gibbs, J. (1994). *Tribes: A new way of learning together.* Santa Rosa, CA: Center Source Publications.

Giroux, H. (1988). *Teachers as intellectuals: Toward a critical pedagogy of learning*. South Hadley, MA: Bergin & Garvey.

Glass ceiling intact. (1995, March 16). *The Sacramento Bee*, pp. A1, A24.

Goldberg, M. (1995). Portrait of John Goodlad. *Educational Leadership, 52*(6), 82–85.

Gramsci, A. (1971). *Selections from the prison notebooks*. London, England: Lawrence & Wishart.

Hanson, D. (1994, August 27). Caring spells career success for teacher. *The Turlock Journal*, pp. A1, A11.

Johnson, D., & Johnson, R. (1987). Research shows the benefits of adult co-operation. *Educational Leadership, 45*(3), 27–30.

Kagan, S. (1990). *Cooperative learning: Resources for teachers*. Riverside: Printing and Repographics, University of California, Riverside.

Kozulin, A. (Ed.). (1986). Vygtosky in context. In L. S. Vygotsky, *Thought and language*, (pp. xi–lvi). Cambridge, MA: MIT Press.

Krashen, S. (1994, October 24). *Second language acquisition*. Syposium for Multidistrict Trainer of Trainer's Institute, San Joaquín County Office of Education, Stockton, CA.

Lankshear, C., & McLaren, P. (Eds.). (1993). *Critical literacy: Politics, praxis, and the postmodern*. Albany: State University of New York Press.

Lieberman, A. (1986). Collaborative research: Working with, not working on. *Educational Leadership, 43*(5), 29–31.

Lindfors, J. (1982). Exploring in and through language. In M. A. Clarke & J. Handscombe (Eds.), *On TESOL '82: Pacific perspectives on language learning and teaching*. Washington, DC: Teachers of English to Speakers of Other Languages.

Macedo, D. (Ed.). (1994). *Literacies of power*. Boulder, CO: Westview Press.

McCaleb, S. P. (1994). *Building communities of learners*. New York: St. Martin's Press.

McLaren, P. (1989). *Life in schools: An introduction to critical pedagogy in the foundations of education*. White Plains, NY: Longman.

McLaren, P. (1994). Critical pedagogy: Constructing an arch of social dreaming and a doorway to hope. In L. Erwin & D. MacLennan (Eds.), *Sociology of education in Canada: Critical perspectives on theory, research & practice* (pp. 137–160). Toronto: Copp Clark Longman.

Moll, L. (Ed.). (1990). *Vygotsky in education: Instructional implications and applications of sociohistorical psychology*. New York: Cambridge University Press.

Oakes, J. (1985). *Keeping track: How schools structure inequality*. New Haven, CT: Yale University Press.

Skutnabb-Kangas, T. (1993, February 10). *Problem posing within the community*. Symposium for Graduate Students, California State University, Stanislaus, Turlock, CA.

Skutnabb-Kangas, T., & Cummins, J. (1988). Concluding remarks: Language for empowerment. In T. Skutnabb-Kangas & J. Cummins (Eds.), *Minority education: From shame to struggle* (pp. 390–394). Philadelphia, PA: Multilingual Matters.

Slavin, R. (1985). *Learning to cooperate, cooperating to learn*. New York: Plenum Press.

Smith, N. J. (1995). Making the invisible visible: Critical pedagogy as a viable means of educating children. In J. Frederickson (Ed.), *Reclaiming our voices: Bilingual education, critical pedagogy & praxis* (pp. 241–252). Ontario, CA: California Association for Bilingual Education.

Vallance, E. (1995). The public curriculum of orderly images. *Educational Researcher, 24*(2), 4–13.

Vygotsky, L. S. (1962). *Thought and language* (E. Hanfmann & G. Vakar, Trans.). Cambridge, MA: MIT Press.

Vygotsky, L. S. (1978). *Mind in society: The development of higher psychological processes*. Cambridge, MA: Harvard University Press.

Wallas, G. (1926). *The art of thought*. New York: Harcourt, Brace and Company.

Wink, J. (1991). *The emergence of the framework for intervention in bilingual education*. Unpublished doctoral disssertation, Texas A&M University, College Station, TX.

Wink, J., & Almanzo, M. (1995). Critical pedagogy: A lens through which we see. In J. Frederickson (Ed.), *Reclaiming our voices: Bilingual education, critical pedagogy & praxis* (pp. 210–223). Ontario, CA: California Association for Bilingual Education.

Wink, J., Putney, L., & Bravo-Lawrence, I. (1994, September/October). Introduction: La voz de Vygotsky. *CABE Newsletter, 17*(2), 10–11, 13–14.

Wink, J., Putney, L., & Bravo-Lawrence, I. (1994, November/December). Lev Vygotsky: Who in the world was he? *CABE Newsletter, 17*(3), 8–9, 19–20.

Wink, J., Putney, L., & Bravo-Lawrence, I. (1995, January/February). Socioculturally learning: What in the world does it mean? *CABE Newsletter, 17*(4), 8–9, 22.

Wink, J., Putney, L., & Bravo-Lawrence, I. (1995, March/April). The zone of proximal development: How in the world do we create it? *CABE Newsletter, 17*(5), 12–13, 24.

Wink, J., Putney, L., & Bravo-Lawrence, I. (1995, May/June). Creating community a la Lev: Why in the world does it matter? *CABE Newsletter, 17*(6), 11, 22–23.

Wink, J., & Swanson, P. (1993, December). Rethinking lesson designs. *CSU, Stanislaus School of Education Journal, 10*(1), 30–35.

Wink, J., & Wu, Y. (1993, September/October). An introduction to critical pedagogy and the classroom teacher. *CABE Newsletter, 16*(2), 11–12.

Wink, J., & Wu, Y. (1993, November/December). Critical pedagogy: What in the world is it? *CABE Newsletter, 16*(3), 5, 24–26.

Wink, J., & Wu, Y. (1994, January/February). Critical pedagogy: Where in the world did it come from? *CABE Newsletter, 16*(4), 5, 18–19, 21, 23.

Wink, J., & Wu, Y. (1994, March/April). Critical pedagogy: How in the world do you do it? *CABE Newsletter, 16*(5), 25, 28, 30.

Wink, J., & Wu, Y. (1994, May/June). Critical pedagogy: Why in the world does it matter? *CABE Newsletter, 16*(6), 12–13, 21.

Index